The Self-Taught Developer's Guide Book

Written By Richard Aragon

Table of Contents

Preface

In today's rapidly evolving technological landscape, the demand for skilled developers continues to grow. Whether you are a novice eager to break into the world of coding or an experienced professional looking to enhance your skills, "The Self-Taught Developer's Guide Book" is designed to be your comprehensive companion on this journey.

The genesis of this book stems from a deep-seated belief that anyone can learn to code, irrespective of their background or formal education. With the right resources, guidance, and dedication, self-taught developers can achieve the same level of proficiency and success as their formally trained counterparts. This book aims to be the only resource you need, providing a structured and holistic approach to learning coding from scratch and advancing to complex, professional-level skills.

Why This Book?

The world of software development is vast and continually evolving. Navigating this terrain without a roadmap can be overwhelming. This book is structured to guide you step-by-step through the essential concepts and practices of modern software development, ensuring that you build a solid foundation before tackling advanced topics. Each chapter is meticulously crafted to build upon the previous ones, creating a cohesive learning experience that is both comprehensive and practical.

What You Will Learn

1. **Foundations of Programming**: Start with the basics of coding, understanding programming languages, and writing your first lines of code.
2. **Data Structures and Algorithms**: Gain a deep understanding of essential data structures and algorithms, which are the building blocks of efficient code.
3. **Web Development**: Learn how to create dynamic and interactive websites using HTML, CSS, JavaScript, and popular frameworks.
4. **Backend Development**: Explore server-side programming, databases, and API development to build robust backend systems.
5. **DevOps and CI/CD**: Master the practices of continuous integration and deployment, along with tools like Docker, Kubernetes, and CI/CD pipelines.
6. **Mobile App Development**: Develop cross-platform mobile applications using frameworks like React Native and Flutter.
7. **Data Engineering**: Understand the principles of data engineering, including data pipelines, batch and stream processing, and orchestration tools.
8. **Machine Learning and AI**: Dive into advanced machine learning techniques, building and deploying sophisticated models.
9. **Cybersecurity**: Learn the essentials of cybersecurity to protect your applications and data from threats.

Who This Book Is For

This book is for anyone who has the curiosity and determination to learn coding and software development. Whether you are a complete beginner or an experienced developer seeking to broaden your skill set, this guide will provide valuable insights and practical knowledge. It is particularly suited for:

- **Aspiring Developers**: Individuals new to coding who want a structured and comprehensive guide to becoming proficient developers.
- **Self-Taught Programmers**: Developers who have learned coding on their own and wish to fill in gaps and gain a more formal understanding of key concepts.
- **Career Changers**: Professionals from other fields looking to transition into a career in software development.
- **Students and Educators**: Learners and teachers who seek a comprehensive resource that covers both foundational and advanced topics in programming and software development.

How to Use This Book

Each chapter of this book builds on the previous ones, so it is recommended to follow the chapters in sequence, especially if you are a beginner. For more experienced readers, chapters can be used as standalone references for specific topics of interest. Practical examples, exercises, and projects are included throughout the book to reinforce learning and provide hands-on experience.

Our Journey Together

Embarking on the journey to become a self-taught developer can be challenging, but it is also incredibly rewarding. This book aims to be more than just a collection of information; it is a guide, a mentor, and a companion. As you progress through the chapters, you will not only gain technical skills but also develop problem-solving abilities, critical thinking, and the confidence to tackle real-world challenges.

Welcome to "The Self-Taught Developer's Guide Book." Let's begin this exciting journey together, and may your path to becoming a proficient and successful developer be enlightening and fulfilling.

Happy coding!

Richard Aragon

Chapter 1: Embarking on Your Coding Journey

Introduction

Welcome to the beginning of your journey into the world of coding! This book is designed to be your comprehensive guide, providing you with the knowledge and tools you need to become a proficient self-taught developer. Whether you are starting from scratch or have some prior experience, this chapter will set the foundation for your learning journey.

Understanding the Basics

Before diving into the technical details, it's essential to understand the basics of what coding is and why it matters. Coding, also known as programming, is the process of creating instructions for computers to follow. These instructions are written in various programming languages, each designed for specific tasks and applications.

Why Learn to Code?

1. **Problem-Solving Skills**: Coding enhances your ability to solve problems systematically.
2. **Career Opportunities**: The demand for skilled developers is high across various industries.
3. **Creativity**: Coding allows you to create applications, websites, and solutions to real-world problems.
4. **Independence**: Being self-taught means you can learn at your own pace and on your own terms.

Setting Up Your Learning Environment

A conducive learning environment is crucial for your success. Here are some steps to get started:

1. **Choose Your Workspace**: Find a quiet, comfortable place where you can focus without interruptions.
2. **Gather Your Tools**: Ensure you have a reliable computer and internet connection. Consider investing in a good keyboard and mouse for comfort.
3. **Install Essential Software**:
   - **Text Editor**: Tools like Visual Studio Code, Sublime Text, or Atom.
   - **Version Control**: Git and GitHub for managing and sharing your code.
   - **Web Browser**: Google Chrome, Firefox, or any modern browser for testing web applications.
   - **Terminal**: Learn to use the command line interface for navigating your file system and running scripts.

Choosing Your First Programming Language

There are many programming languages to choose from, each with its strengths and use cases. Here are some popular languages for beginners:

1. **Python**: Known for its simplicity and readability, Python is great for web development, data analysis, and automation.
2. **JavaScript**: The language of the web, JavaScript is essential for front-end and back-end web development.
3. **Ruby**: Known for its elegant syntax, Ruby is popular for web development, particularly with the Ruby on Rails framework.

How to Choose?

- **Interest and Goals**: Consider what type of projects you are interested in. For web development, JavaScript is a must. For data science, Python is preferred.
- **Community and Resources**: Look for languages with a strong community and plenty of learning resources.

Setting Realistic Goals

Learning to code is a marathon, not a sprint. Setting realistic and achievable goals will keep you motivated. Here are some tips:

1. **Start Small**: Begin with small, manageable projects that gradually increase in complexity.
2. **Consistent Practice**: Dedicate a specific amount of time each day or week to coding.
3. **Break Down Projects**: Divide your projects into smaller tasks and milestones.
4. **Celebrate Milestones**: Acknowledge and celebrate your progress to stay motivated.

Finding Learning Resources

There are numerous resources available for self-taught developers. Here are some recommended types of resources:

1. **Online Courses**: Platforms like Coursera, Udemy, and Codecademy offer comprehensive courses on various programming languages and technologies.
2. **Books**: "Automate the Boring Stuff with Python" by Al Sweigart and "Eloquent JavaScript" by Marijn Haverbeke are excellent starting points.
3. **Documentation**: Official documentation and tutorials are invaluable for learning the specifics of a language or framework.
4. **Communities**: Join online forums, social media groups, and local meetups to connect with other learners and experienced developers.

Practical Exercise: Your First Code

Let's write your first piece of code. We'll start with a simple "Hello, World!" program in Python. Follow these steps:

1. **Open Your Text Editor**: Launch your preferred text editor.

Write the Code: Type the following code:

```
print("Hello, World!")
```

2.
3. **Save the File**: Save the file with a `.py` extension, for example, `hello.py`.

Run the Code: Open your terminal, navigate to the directory where you saved the file, and run the following command:

```
python hello.py
```

4.
5. **See the Output**: You should see "Hello, World!" printed in the terminal.

Conclusion

Congratulations! You've just written and executed your first program. This is the beginning of your journey into the world of coding. As you continue, remember to stay curious, practice consistently, and seek help when needed. The path to becoming a self-taught developer is challenging but immensely rewarding.

In the next chapter, we will dive deeper into the fundamentals of programming, exploring variables, data types, and basic syntax. Keep up the great work, and let's move forward together!

Chapter 2: Fundamentals of Programming

Introduction

Now that you've set up your environment and written your first "Hello, World!" program, it's time to dive deeper into the fundamentals of programming. Understanding these core concepts is essential as they form the foundation for everything you'll do as a developer.

Variables and Data Types

What is a Variable?

A variable is a storage location in your computer's memory that holds a value. This value can change throughout the execution of your program, hence the name "variable."

Naming Variables

When naming variables, follow these rules:

- Use meaningful names that describe the data they hold.
- Start with a letter or underscore, followed by letters, numbers, or underscores.
- Avoid using reserved keywords (words that have special meaning in the language).

Examples:

```
# Valid variable names

age = 25

name = "Alice"

_is_valid = True


# Invalid variable names

1name = "Alice"  # Starts with a number

class = "Physics"  # Reserved keyword
```

Common Data Types

Integers: Whole numbers without a decimal point.

```
age = 25
```

    1.

Floats: Numbers with a decimal point.

```
price = 19.99
```

    2.

Strings: Text enclosed in quotes.

```
name = "Alice"
```

    3.

Booleans: Representing `True` or `False`.

```
is_student = True
```

    4.

Basic Operations

Arithmetic Operations

You can perform arithmetic operations on numerical data types.

```
a = 10

b = 3


# Addition

sum = a + b   # 13


# Subtraction

difference = a - b   # 7
```

```
# Multiplication

product = a * b  # 30


# Division

quotient = a / b  # 3.3333...


# Integer Division

int_quotient = a // b  # 3


# Modulus

remainder = a % b  # 1


# Exponentiation

power = a ** b  # 1000
```

String Operations

Strings can be concatenated and manipulated using various operations.

```
first_name = "Alice"

last_name = "Smith"


# Concatenation

full_name = first_name + " " + last_name  # "Alice Smith"
```

```
# Repetition

repeated_name = first_name * 3  # "AliceAliceAlice"
```

Control Structures

Conditional Statements

Conditional statements allow your program to make decisions based on certain conditions.

```
age = 18
```

```
if age >= 18:

    print("You are an adult.")

else:

    print("You are a minor.")
```

You can also use `elif` for multiple conditions.

```
score = 85
```

```
if score >= 90:

    grade = "A"

elif score >= 80:

    grade = "B"

elif score >= 70:

    grade = "C"

elif score >= 60:
```

```python
    grade = "D"
else:
    grade = "F"
```

Loops

Loops allow you to repeat a block of code multiple times.

For Loop

```python
# Print numbers from 0 to 4
for i in range(5):
    print(i)
```

While Loop

```python
# Print numbers from 0 to 4
i = 0
while i < 5:
    print(i)
    i += 1
```

Functions

Functions are reusable blocks of code that perform a specific task. They help you organize your code and make it more readable.

Defining and Calling Functions

```python
def greet(name):
    print("Hello, " + name + "!")
```

```
greet("Alice")  # Output: Hello, Alice!
```

Return Values

Functions can return values using the `return` statement.

```
def add(a, b):

    return a + b
```

```
result = add(3, 5)  # result is 8
```

Practical Exercise: Build a Simple Calculator

Let's build a simple calculator that can perform basic arithmetic operations.

1. **Define the Functions**

```
def add(a, b):

    return a + b
```

```
def subtract(a, b):

    return a - b
```

```
def multiply(a, b):

    return a * b
```

```
def divide(a, b):
```

```python
    if b != 0:
        return a / b
    else:
        return "Error: Division by zero"
```

2. Create a User Interface

```python
def calculator():
    print("Simple Calculator")
    print("Select operation:")
    print("1. Add")
    print("2. Subtract")
    print("3. Multiply")
    print("4. Divide")

    choice = input("Enter choice (1/2/3/4): ")

    num1 = float(input("Enter first number: "))
    num2 = float(input("Enter second number: "))

    if choice == '1':
        print("Result:", add(num1, num2))
    elif choice == '2':
        print("Result:", subtract(num1, num2))
```

```
    elif choice == '3':

        print("Result:", multiply(num1, num2))

    elif choice == '4':

        print("Result:", divide(num1, num2))

    else:

        print("Invalid input")


calculator()
```

Conclusion

In this chapter, we've covered the fundamental concepts of programming, including variables, data types, basic operations, control structures, and functions. These are the building blocks for writing more complex and powerful programs. Practice these concepts by writing small programs and experimenting with different operations and structures.

In the next chapter, we will explore data structures, which are essential for organizing and managing data efficiently in your programs. Keep practicing and building your skills—you're on your way to becoming a proficient self-taught developer!

Chapter 3: Mastering Data Structures

Introduction

Data structures are fundamental components in programming that allow you to store, organize, and manipulate data efficiently. Mastering these structures is crucial for writing effective and optimized code. In this chapter, we'll explore some of the most common data structures, including lists, tuples, dictionaries, and sets.

Lists

What is a List?

A list is a collection of items in a particular order. Lists can hold items of any data type and are mutable, meaning their contents can be changed.

Creating Lists

```
# Creating a list

numbers = [1, 2, 3, 4, 5]

names = ["Alice", "Bob", "Charlie"]

mixed = [1, "Alice", 3.5, True]
```

Accessing Elements

```
# Accessing elements by index

print(numbers[0])   # Output: 1

print(names[2])     # Output: Charlie


# Negative indexing

print(numbers[-1])  # Output: 5 (last element)
```

Modifying Lists

```python
# Changing elements
numbers[0] = 10
print(numbers)  # Output: [10, 2, 3, 4, 5]


# Adding elements
numbers.append(6)
print(numbers)  # Output: [10, 2, 3, 4, 5, 6]


# Inserting elements
numbers.insert(1, 15)
print(numbers)  # Output: [10, 15, 2, 3, 4, 5, 6]


# Removing elements
numbers.remove(15)
print(numbers)  # Output: [10, 2, 3, 4, 5, 6]
```

List Operations

```python
# Length of a list
print(len(numbers))  # Output: 6


# Slicing
print(numbers[1:4])  # Output: [2, 3, 4]
```

```
# Checking if an item exists

print(4 in numbers)  # Output: True
```

Tuples

What is a Tuple?

A tuple is similar to a list, but it is immutable, meaning once it is created, its contents cannot be changed.

Creating Tuples

```
# Creating a tuple

coordinates = (10, 20)

names = ("Alice", "Bob", "Charlie")
```

Accessing Elements

```
# Accessing elements by index

print(coordinates[0])  # Output: 10

print(names[2])         # Output: Charlie
```

```
# Negative indexing

print(coordinates[-1])  # Output: 20 (last element)
```

Tuples vs Lists

- **Mutability**: Lists are mutable, tuples are immutable.
- **Use Cases**: Tuples are used when the data should not change, such as coordinates, fixed settings, etc.

Dictionaries

What is a Dictionary?

A dictionary is a collection of key-value pairs, where each key is unique. Dictionaries are mutable and allow for fast retrieval of data based on keys.

Creating Dictionaries

```
# Creating a dictionary
person = {
    "name": "Alice",
    "age": 25,
    "city": "New York"
}
```

Accessing Elements

```
# Accessing elements by key
print(person["name"])   # Output: Alice


# Adding or modifying elements
person["age"] = 26
person["job"] = "Engineer"
print(person)   # Output: {'name': 'Alice', 'age': 26, 'city': 'New York', 'job': 'Engineer'}


# Removing elements
del person["city"]
```

```python
print(person)  # Output: {'name': 'Alice', 'age': 26, 'job':
'Engineer'}
```

Dictionary Operations

```python
# Length of a dictionary

print(len(person))  # Output: 3


# Checking if a key exists

print("name" in person)  # Output: True


# Iterating over keys and values

for key, value in person.items():

    print(key, value)
```

Sets

What is a Set?

A set is a collection of unique items. Sets are unordered and do not allow duplicate elements.

Creating Sets

```python
# Creating a set

fruits = {"apple", "banana", "cherry"}
```

Modifying Sets

```python
# Adding elements

fruits.add("orange")
```

```python
print(fruits)  # Output: {'orange', 'apple', 'banana', 'cherry'}


# Removing elements
fruits.remove("banana")
print(fruits)  # Output: {'orange', 'apple', 'cherry'}
```

Set Operations

```python
# Length of a set
print(len(fruits))  # Output: 3


# Checking if an item exists
print("apple" in fruits)  # Output: True


# Set operations
set1 = {1, 2, 3}
set2 = {3, 4, 5}


# Union
print(set1 | set2)  # Output: {1, 2, 3, 4, 5}


# Intersection
print(set1 & set2)  # Output: {3}
```

```
# Difference

print(set1 - set2)   # Output: {1, 2}
```

Practical Exercise: Contact List Application

Let's build a simple contact list application using the data structures we have learned.

1. **Define the Contact List**

```
contacts = {
    "Alice": {"phone": "123-456-7890", "email": "alice@example.com"},
    "Bob": {"phone": "987-654-3210", "email": "bob@example.com"}
}
```

2. **Functions to Manage Contacts**

```
def add_contact(name, phone, email):
    contacts[name] = {"phone": phone, "email": email}


def remove_contact(name):
    if name in contacts:
        del contacts[name]
    else:
        print("Contact not found.")


def update_contact(name, phone=None, email=None):
    if name in contacts:
```

```python
        if phone:

            contacts[name]["phone"] = phone

        if email:

            contacts[name]["email"] = email

    else:

        print("Contact not found.")


def display_contacts():

    for name, info in contacts.items():

        print(f"Name: {name}, Phone: {info['phone']}, Email:
{info['email']}")
```

3. Interactive Menu

```python
def contact_list_app():

    while True:

        print("\nContact List Application")

        print("1. Add Contact")

        print("2. Remove Contact")

        print("3. Update Contact")

        print("4. Display Contacts")

        print("5. Exit")


        choice = input("Enter choice (1/2/3/4/5): ")
```

```python
        if choice == '1':
            name = input("Enter name: ")
            phone = input("Enter phone number: ")
            email = input("Enter email: ")
            add_contact(name, phone, email)
        elif choice == '2':
            name = input("Enter name: ")
            remove_contact(name)
        elif choice == '3':
            name = input("Enter name: ")
            phone = input("Enter phone number (leave blank to keep
current): ")
            email = input("Enter email (leave blank to keep current):
")
            update_contact(name, phone or None, email or None)
        elif choice == '4':
            display_contacts()
        elif choice == '5':
            break
        else:
            print("Invalid choice, please try again.")
```

```
contact_list_app()
```

Conclusion

In this chapter, we covered essential data structures including lists, tuples, dictionaries, and sets. Understanding and utilizing these structures will significantly improve your ability to handle and manipulate data in your programs. Practice creating and working with these data structures to reinforce your understanding.

In the next chapter, we will delve into object-oriented programming (OOP), which will further enhance your ability to design and structure complex programs. Keep up the great work, and let's continue building your skills together!

Chapter 4: Object-Oriented Programming

Introduction

Object-Oriented Programming (OOP) is a programming paradigm that uses objects and classes to structure and organize code. OOP makes it easier to manage and manipulate complex data structures and enhances code reusability and maintainability. In this chapter, we'll explore the fundamentals of OOP, including classes, objects, inheritance, and polymorphism.

Understanding Classes and Objects

What is a Class?

A class is a blueprint for creating objects. It defines a set of attributes and methods that the objects created from the class will have.

What is an Object?

An object is an instance of a class. It contains data (attributes) and functions (methods) defined by the class.

Defining a Class

Let's start by defining a simple class in Python.

```python
class Dog:

    def __init__(self, name, age):

        self.name = name

        self.age = age


    def bark(self):

        print(f"{self.name} is barking.")


    def get_age(self):

        return self.age
```

Creating Objects

Once you have a class, you can create objects from it.

```python
# Creating objects

dog1 = Dog("Buddy", 3)

dog2 = Dog("Max", 5)


# Accessing attributes and methods

print(dog1.name)  # Output: Buddy

print(dog1.get_age())  # Output: 3

dog1.bark()  # Output: Buddy is barking.
```

Inheritance

Inheritance allows you to create a new class based on an existing class. The new class inherits the attributes and methods of the existing class.

Defining a Subclass

Let's define a subclass that inherits from the Dog class.

```python
class GuideDog(Dog):

    def __init__(self, name, age, guide_for):

        super().__init__(name, age)

        self.guide_for = guide_for


    def guide(self):
```

```
        print(f"{self.name} is guiding {self.guide_for}.")
```

Creating Subclass Objects

```
# Creating objects

guide_dog = GuideDog("Rex", 4, "Alice")


# Accessing attributes and methods from both the superclass and
subclass

print(guide_dog.name)  # Output: Rex

print(guide_dog.get_age())  # Output: 4

guide_dog.bark()  # Output: Rex is barking.

guide_dog.guide()  # Output: Rex is guiding Alice.
```

Polymorphism

Polymorphism allows you to define methods in a superclass and override them in a subclass, enabling you to use the same method name in different contexts.

Method Overriding

```
class Animal:

    def sound(self):

        print("This animal makes a sound.")


class Cat(Animal):

    def sound(self):

        print("The cat meows.")
```

```
class Dog(Animal):

    def sound(self):

        print("The dog barks.")


# Using polymorphism

animals = [Cat(), Dog()]


for animal in animals:

    animal.sound()
```

Encapsulation

Encapsulation is the practice of hiding the internal state and behavior of an object and only exposing a public interface. This is achieved using access modifiers.

Private Attributes and Methods

```
class Person:

    def __init__(self, name, age):

        self._name = name   # Protected attribute

        self.__age = age   # Private attribute


    def get_age(self):

        return self.__age
```

```python
    def _display_name(self):

        print(f"Name: {self._name}")


# Creating an object

person = Person("Alice", 30)


# Accessing protected and private attributes

print(person._name)  # Output: Alice (Not recommended)

print(person.get_age())  # Output: 30

# print(person.__age)  # AttributeError: 'Person' object has no
attribute '__age'
```

Practical Exercise: Bank Account Management System

Let's build a simple bank account management system using the concepts of OOP.

1. **Define the Account Class**

```python
class Account:

    def __init__(self, owner, balance=0):

        self.owner = owner

        self.balance = balance


    def deposit(self, amount):

        self.balance += amount

        print(f"Deposited {amount}. New balance: {self.balance}")
```

```python
    def withdraw(self, amount):

        if amount > self.balance:

            print("Insufficient funds.")

        else:

            self.balance -= amount

            print(f"Withdrew {amount}. New balance: {self.balance}")


    def get_balance(self):

        return self.balance
```

2. Define the SavingsAccount Subclass

```python
class SavingsAccount(Account):

    def __init__(self, owner, balance=0, interest_rate=0.02):

        super().__init__(owner, balance)

        self.interest_rate = interest_rate


    def apply_interest(self):

        interest = self.balance * self.interest_rate

        self.balance += interest

        print(f"Applied interest: {interest}. New balance: {self.balance}")
```

3. Create an Interactive Menu

```python
def bank_system():

    accounts = {}


    while True:

        print("\nBank Account Management System")

        print("1. Create Account")

        print("2. Deposit")

        print("3. Withdraw")

        print("4. Apply Interest (Savings Account)")

        print("5. Check Balance")

        print("6. Exit")


        choice = input("Enter choice (1/2/3/4/5/6): ")


        if choice == '1':

            owner = input("Enter account owner: ")

            acc_type = input("Enter account type (regular/savings): ")

            if acc_type.lower() == "savings":

                account = SavingsAccount(owner)

            else:

                account = Account(owner)

            accounts[owner] = account
```

```python
            print(f"Account created for {owner}.")
    elif choice == '2':
        owner = input("Enter account owner: ")
        amount = float(input("Enter amount to deposit: "))
        if owner in accounts:
            accounts[owner].deposit(amount)
        else:
            print("Account not found.")
    elif choice == '3':
        owner = input("Enter account owner: ")
        amount = float(input("Enter amount to withdraw: "))
        if owner in accounts:
            accounts[owner].withdraw(amount)
        else:
            print("Account not found.")
    elif choice == '4':
        owner = input("Enter account owner: ")
        if owner in accounts and isinstance(accounts[owner],
SavingsAccount):
            accounts[owner].apply_interest()
        else:
            print("Savings account not found.")
    elif choice == '5':
```

```python
        owner = input("Enter account owner: ")

        if owner in accounts:

            print(f"Balance: {accounts[owner].get_balance()}")

        else:

            print("Account not found.")

    elif choice == '6':

        break

    else:

        print("Invalid choice, please try again.")


bank_system()
```

Conclusion

In this chapter, we covered the core principles of Object-Oriented Programming, including classes, objects, inheritance, polymorphism, and encapsulation. Understanding these concepts will enable you to design and implement more complex and maintainable code. Practice these principles by creating your own classes and objects and experimenting with inheritance and polymorphism.

In the next chapter, we will delve into error handling and debugging, which are essential skills for writing robust and error-free code. Keep up the great work, and let's continue your journey to becoming a proficient self-taught developer!

Chapter 5: Error Handling and Debugging

Introduction

No matter how experienced you become as a developer, errors and bugs are inevitable. Knowing how to handle errors gracefully and debug your code efficiently is crucial to creating robust and reliable applications. In this chapter, we'll explore error handling techniques, debugging tools, and best practices to help you tackle issues effectively.

Types of Errors

Before diving into error handling and debugging, it's essential to understand the different types of errors you might encounter:

1. **Syntax Errors**: Mistakes in the code's structure that prevent it from running.
2. **Runtime Errors**: Errors that occur while the program is running, often due to invalid operations or conditions.
3. **Logical Errors**: Errors in the logic of the code that cause it to behave incorrectly.

Handling Errors with Exceptions

What is an Exception?

An exception is an event that disrupts the normal flow of a program. Python provides a way to handle these exceptions using `try`, `except`, `else`, and `finally` blocks.

Basic Exception Handling

```
try:

    # Code that may raise an exception

    result = 10 / 0

except ZeroDivisionError:

    # Code to handle the exception

    print("Error: Division by zero is not allowed.")
```

Multiple Exceptions

You can handle multiple exceptions by specifying them in separate `except` blocks.

```python
try:

    number = int(input("Enter a number: "))

    result = 10 / number

except ValueError:

    print("Error: Invalid input. Please enter a valid number.")

except ZeroDivisionError:

    print("Error: Division by zero is not allowed.")
```

Else and Finally

The else block runs if no exceptions are raised, and the finally block runs regardless of whether an exception was raised.

```python
try:

    number = int(input("Enter a number: "))

    result = 10 / number

except ValueError:

    print("Error: Invalid input. Please enter a valid number.")

except ZeroDivisionError:

    print("Error: Division by zero is not allowed.")

else:

    print(f"The result is {result}.")

finally:

    print("Execution completed.")
```

Raising Exceptions

You can raise exceptions intentionally using the `raise` keyword.

```python
def check_age(age):

    if age < 0:

        raise ValueError("Age cannot be negative.")

    print(f"Age is {age}.")


try:

    check_age(-1)

except ValueError as e:

    print(f"Error: {e}")
```

Debugging Techniques

Debugging is the process of identifying and fixing errors in your code. Here are some common debugging techniques:

Print Statements

Using print statements to output the values of variables and the flow of execution can help you identify where things go wrong.

```python
def divide(a, b):

    print(f"Dividing {a} by {b}")

    result = a / b

    print(f"Result is {result}")

    return result
```

```
divide(10, 0)
```

Using a Debugger

A debugger allows you to step through your code line by line, inspect variables, and evaluate expressions. Most modern IDEs come with built-in debuggers. For example, Visual Studio Code has a powerful debugging tool.

1. **Set Breakpoints**: Click next to the line numbers to set breakpoints.
2. **Start Debugging**: Run the debugger to start your program.
3. **Step Through Code**: Use the controls to step over, into, or out of functions.
4. **Inspect Variables**: Hover over variables to see their current values.

Logging

Logging provides a way to track events that happen during the execution of a program. The Python `logging` module allows you to record messages to a file or console with different levels of severity.

```
import logging


logging.basicConfig(level=logging.DEBUG, filename='app.log',
filemode='w', format='%(name)s - %(levelname)s - %(message)s')


logging.debug('This is a debug message')

logging.info('This is an info message')

logging.warning('This is a warning message')

logging.error('This is an error message')

logging.critical('This is a critical message')
```

Practical Exercise: Debugging a Simple Application

Let's debug a simple application that calculates the factorial of a number.

1. The Problematic Code

```
def factorial(n):

    if n == 0:

        return 1

    else:

        return n * factorial(n - 1)


number = int(input("Enter a number: "))

print(f"The factorial of {number} is {factorial(number)}.")
```

2. Introduce a Bug

Modify the code to introduce a bug:

```
def factorial(n):

    if n == 0:

        return 1

    else:

        return n * factorial(n)   # Incorrect recursive call


number = int(input("Enter a number: "))

print(f"The factorial of {number} is {factorial(number)}.")
```

3. Debug the Code

Use the following steps to debug the code:

- **Add print statements:**

```python
def factorial(n):

    print(f"Calculating factorial of {n}")

    if n == 0:

        return 1

    else:

        return n * factorial(n)  # Incorrect recursive call


number = int(input("Enter a number: "))
print(f"The factorial of {number} is {factorial(number)}.")
```

- **Identify the issue and fix the code:**

```python
def factorial(n):

    print(f"Calculating factorial of {n}")

    if n == 0:

        return 1

    else:

        return n * factorial(n - 1)  # Correct recursive call


number = int(input("Enter a number: "))
print(f"The factorial of {number} is {factorial(number)}.")
```

Conclusion

In this chapter, we covered the essential techniques for handling errors and debugging your code. Proper error handling ensures your programs can deal with unexpected situations gracefully, while effective debugging helps you identify and resolve issues quickly. Practice these techniques to become proficient in writing robust and error-free code.

In the next chapter, we will explore working with external libraries and APIs, which will expand the functionality of your programs and enable you to build more sophisticated applications. Keep up the excellent work, and let's continue your journey to becoming a proficient self-taught developer!

Chapter 6: Working with External Libraries and APIs

Introduction

External libraries and APIs (Application Programming Interfaces) can significantly enhance the functionality of your programs by allowing you to leverage pre-built code and interact with external services. In this chapter, we'll explore how to install and use external libraries, as well as how to interact with APIs to fetch and manipulate data.

Installing and Using External Libraries

What are External Libraries?

External libraries are collections of pre-written code that you can use to add functionality to your programs without having to write the code from scratch. Python has a vast ecosystem of libraries available through the Python Package Index (PyPI).

Installing Libraries with pip

The `pip` tool is used to install external libraries. To install a library, use the following command:

```
pip install library_name
```

For example, to install the popular `requests` library for making HTTP requests:

```
pip install requests
```

Importing and Using Libraries

Once installed, you can import and use the library in your code.

```python
import requests


response = requests.get("https://api.github.com")

print(response.status_code)  # Output: 200

print(response.json())  # Output: JSON data from GitHub API
```

Interacting with APIs

APIs allow you to interact with external services and data sources. You can use APIs to fetch data, send data, and perform various operations. APIs often use HTTP requests to communicate between the client and server.

Understanding HTTP Methods

- **GET**: Retrieve data from the server.
- **POST**: Send data to the server.
- **PUT**: Update existing data on the server.
- **DELETE**: Delete data from the server.

Making GET Requests

The `requests` library makes it easy to make HTTP requests. Here's how to make a GET request:

```python
import requests


url = "https://api.github.com/users/octocat"

response = requests.get(url)


if response.status_code == 200:

    data = response.json()

    print(data)
else:

    print(f"Failed to retrieve data: {response.status_code}")
```

Making POST Requests

To send data to an API, you can use a POST request. Here's an example:

```python
import requests
```

```python
url = "https://jsonplaceholder.typicode.com/posts"

payload = {

    "title": "foo",

    "body": "bar",

    "userId": 1

}

response = requests.post(url, json=payload)


if response.status_code == 201:

    data = response.json()

    print(data)

else:

    print(f"Failed to send data: {response.status_code}")
```

Handling API Responses

API responses often come in JSON format. You can parse and manipulate this data in your Python code.

Parsing JSON Data

```python
import requests


url = "https://api.github.com/users/octocat"

response = requests.get(url)
```

```python
if response.status_code == 200:

    data = response.json()

    print(f"User: {data['login']}")

    print(f"Name: {data['name']}")

    print(f"Public Repos: {data['public_repos']}")

else:

    print(f"Failed to retrieve data: {response.status_code}")
```

Practical Exercise: Weather App

Let's build a simple weather application that fetches weather data from an API and displays it to the user.

1. **Sign Up for an API Key**

First, sign up for an API key from a weather API provider, such as OpenWeatherMap.

2. **Fetch Weather Data**

```python
import requests


api_key = "your_api_key_here"

city = "London"

url =
f"http://api.openweathermap.org/data/2.5/weather?q={city}&appid={api_k
ey}"


response = requests.get(url)
```

```python
if response.status_code == 200:
    data = response.json()
    main = data['main']
    temperature = main['temp']
    pressure = main['pressure']
    humidity = main['humidity']
    weather = data['weather'][0]['description']

    print(f"City: {city}")
    print(f"Temperature: {temperature}")
    print(f"Pressure: {pressure}")
    print(f"Humidity: {humidity}")
    print(f"Weather Description: {weather}")
else:
    print(f"Failed to retrieve data: {response.status_code}")
```

3. Convert Temperature

The temperature is often returned in Kelvin. Convert it to Celsius or Fahrenheit:

```python
def kelvin_to_celsius(kelvin):
    return kelvin - 273.15


temperature_celsius = kelvin_to_celsius(temperature)
```

```
print(f"Temperature in Celsius: {temperature_celsius:.2f}")
```

4. Interactive Weather App

Enhance the app to take user input for the city:

```python
import requests


def get_weather(api_key, city):
    url =
f"http://api.openweathermap.org/data/2.5/weather?q={city}&appid={api_k
ey}"

    response = requests.get(url)

    if response.status_code == 200:

        return response.json()

    else:

        print(f"Failed to retrieve data: {response.status_code}")

        return None


def kelvin_to_celsius(kelvin):

    return kelvin - 273.15


def display_weather(data):

    main = data['main']

    temperature = kelvin_to_celsius(main['temp'])

    pressure = main['pressure']
```

```python
    humidity = main['humidity']

    weather = data['weather'][0]['description']


    print(f"Temperature: {temperature:.2f}°C")

    print(f"Pressure: {pressure} hPa")

    print(f"Humidity: {humidity}%")

    print(f"Weather Description: {weather}")


def weather_app():

    api_key = "your_api_key_here"

    city = input("Enter city name: ")

    data = get_weather(api_key, city)

    if data:

        display_weather(data)


weather_app()
```

Conclusion

In this chapter, we covered how to install and use external libraries and interact with APIs. These skills are essential for expanding the functionality of your programs and integrating with external services. Practice making API requests and handling responses to become comfortable working with various APIs.

In the next chapter, we will explore databases and how to manage data storage for your applications. Keep up the excellent work, and let's continue your journey to becoming a proficient self-taught developer!

Chapter 7: Managing Data with Databases

Introduction

Databases are essential for storing, managing, and retrieving large amounts of data efficiently. Understanding how to work with databases is crucial for any developer. In this chapter, we will explore the basics of relational databases, how to use SQL (Structured Query Language) to interact with databases, and how to integrate databases into your Python applications.

Relational Databases

What is a Relational Database?

A relational database organizes data into tables, which consist of rows and columns. Each table represents an entity, and relationships between tables are established using keys.

Common Relational Database Systems

- **SQLite**: Lightweight and file-based, suitable for small applications.
- **MySQL**: Popular open-source database, widely used in web applications.
- **PostgreSQL**: Advanced open-source database with support for complex queries and data types.

SQL Basics

SQL is the standard language for interacting with relational databases. Here are some fundamental SQL operations:

Creating a Table

```
CREATE TABLE users (

    id INTEGER PRIMARY KEY AUTOINCREMENT,

    name TEXT NOT NULL,

    email TEXT UNIQUE NOT NULL,

    age INTEGER

);
```

Inserting Data

```
INSERT INTO users (name, email, age) VALUES ('Alice',
'alice@example.com', 30);
```

Querying Data

```
SELECT * FROM users;
```

Updating Data

```
UPDATE users SET age = 31 WHERE name = 'Alice';
```

Deleting Data

```
DELETE FROM users WHERE name = 'Alice';
```

Integrating Databases with Python

Python provides several libraries to work with databases. We'll focus on SQLite, which is easy to use and doesn't require a separate server.

Using SQLite with Python

1. Installing SQLite

SQLite comes pre-installed with Python. If you need to install it separately, you can do so using pip:

```
pip install pysqlite3
```

2. Connecting to a Database

```
import sqlite3
```

```python
# Connect to a database (or create it if it doesn't exist)
conn = sqlite3.connect('example.db')


# Create a cursor object
cursor = conn.cursor()
```

3. Creating a Table

```python
cursor.execute('''CREATE TABLE users
                  (id INTEGER PRIMARY KEY AUTOINCREMENT,
                   name TEXT NOT NULL,
                   email TEXT UNIQUE NOT NULL,
                   age INTEGER)''')
conn.commit()
```

4. Inserting Data

```python
cursor.execute("INSERT INTO users (name, email, age) VALUES (?, ?, ?)",
               ('Alice', 'alice@example.com', 30))
conn.commit()
```

5. Querying Data

```python
cursor.execute("SELECT * FROM users")
rows = cursor.fetchall()
```

```
for row in rows:

    print(row)
```

6. Updating Data

```
cursor.execute("UPDATE users SET age = ? WHERE name = ?", (31,
'Alice'))

conn.commit()
```

7. Deleting Data

```
cursor.execute("DELETE FROM users WHERE name = ?", ('Alice',))

conn.commit()
```

8. Closing the Connection

```
conn.close()
```

Practical Exercise: Task Manager Application

Let's build a simple task manager application that allows users to add, view, update, and delete tasks.

1. Define the Database Schema

```
import sqlite3


def create_connection():

    conn = sqlite3.connect('tasks.db')
```

```python
    return conn


def create_table(conn):

    cursor = conn.cursor()

    cursor.execute('''CREATE TABLE IF NOT EXISTS tasks

                        (id INTEGER PRIMARY KEY AUTOINCREMENT,

                         title TEXT NOT NULL,

                         description TEXT,

                         status TEXT NOT NULL)''')

    conn.commit()


conn = create_connection()

create_table(conn)

conn.close()
```

2. **Add Task Function**

```python
def add_task(conn, title, description, status):

    cursor = conn.cursor()

    cursor.execute("INSERT INTO tasks (title, description, status)
VALUES (?, ?, ?)",

                    (title, description, status))

    conn.commit()
```

3. View Tasks Function

```
def view_tasks(conn):

    cursor = conn.cursor()

    cursor.execute("SELECT * FROM tasks")

    rows = cursor.fetchall()

    return rows
```

4. Update Task Function

```
def update_task(conn, task_id, title, description, status):

    cursor = conn.cursor()

    cursor.execute("UPDATE tasks SET title = ?, description = ?,
status = ? WHERE id = ?",

                    (title, description, status, task_id))

    conn.commit()
```

5. Delete Task Function

```
def delete_task(conn, task_id):

    cursor = conn.cursor()

    cursor.execute("DELETE FROM tasks WHERE id = ?", (task_id,))

    conn.commit()
```

6. Interactive Task Manager Application

```
def task_manager():

    conn = create_connection()
```

```python
    create_table(conn)

    while True:
        print("\nTask Manager")
        print("1. Add Task")
        print("2. View Tasks")
        print("3. Update Task")
        print("4. Delete Task")
        print("5. Exit")

        choice = input("Enter choice (1/2/3/4/5): ")

        if choice == '1':
            title = input("Enter task title: ")
            description = input("Enter task description: ")
            status = input("Enter task status: ")
            add_task(conn, title, description, status)
        elif choice == '2':
            tasks = view_tasks(conn)
            for task in tasks:
                print(task)
        elif choice == '3':
            task_id = int(input("Enter task ID: "))
```

```python
        title = input("Enter new task title: ")

        description = input("Enter new task description: ")

        status = input("Enter new task status: ")

        update_task(conn, task_id, title, description, status)
    elif choice == '4':

        task_id = int(input("Enter task ID: "))

        delete_task(conn, task_id)
    elif choice == '5':

        break

    else:

        print("Invalid choice, please try again.")


    conn.close()


task_manager()
```

Conclusion

In this chapter, we covered the basics of relational databases, how to use SQL to interact with databases, and how to integrate databases into your Python applications. Working with databases is a critical skill for any developer, as it enables you to store, manage, and retrieve data efficiently.

In the next chapter, we will explore web development, including how to create dynamic websites and web applications. Keep practicing, and let's continue your journey to becoming a proficient self-taught developer!

Chapter 8: Introduction to Web Development

Introduction

Web development is the process of creating websites and web applications that run on the internet. It encompasses various technologies and frameworks to build dynamic and interactive user experiences. In this chapter, we will explore the basics of web development, including HTML, CSS, JavaScript, and how to create a simple web application using Python and Flask.

The Building Blocks of the Web

HTML (HyperText Markup Language)

HTML is the standard markup language used to create web pages. It defines the structure of a webpage using elements and tags.

```
<!DOCTYPE html>

<html>

<head>

    <title>My First Web Page</title>

</head>

<body>

    <h1>Welcome to My Website</h1>

    <p>This is a paragraph.</p>

    <a href="https://www.example.com">Visit Example</a>

</body>

</html>
```

CSS (Cascading Style Sheets)

CSS is used to style and layout web pages. It controls the visual appearance of HTML elements.

```html
<!DOCTYPE html>

<html>

<head>

    <title>Styled Web Page</title>

    <style>

        body {

            font-family: Arial, sans-serif;

        }

        h1 {

            color: blue;

        }

        p {

            color: green;

        }

    </style>

</head>

<body>

    <h1>Welcome to My Styled Website</h1>

    <p>This is a styled paragraph.</p>

</body>

</html>
```

JavaScript

JavaScript is a programming language that adds interactivity to web pages. It can be used to manipulate the DOM (Document Object Model), handle events, and create dynamic content.

```html
<!DOCTYPE html>

<html>

<head>

    <title>Interactive Web Page</title>

    <script>

        function showMessage() {

            alert("Hello, welcome to my website!");

        }

    </script>

</head>

<body>

    <h1>Interactive Web Page</h1>

    <button onclick="showMessage()">Click Me</button>

</body>

</html>
```

Introduction to Flask

Flask is a lightweight web framework for Python that allows you to build web applications quickly and easily.

Installing Flask

To get started with Flask, you need to install it using pip:

```
pip install flask
```

Creating a Simple Web Application

1. **Hello World Application**

```python
from flask import Flask


app = Flask(__name__)


@app.route('/')
def hello_world():
    return 'Hello, World!'


if __name__ == '__main__':
    app.run(debug=True)
```

Save this code in a file named `app.py`, and run it using:

```
python app.py
```

Visit `http://127.0.0.1:5000/` in your web browser to see the result.

2. Adding Routes

Routes define the different pages of your web application.

```
from flask import Flask


app = Flask(__name__)


@app.route('/')
def home():
    return 'Welcome to the Home Page!'


@app.route('/about')
def about():
    return 'About Page'


if __name__ == '__main__':
    app.run(debug=True)
```

3. Using Templates

Templates allow you to create dynamic HTML content. Flask uses Jinja2 templating engine.

Create a folder named templates and add a file named index.html:

```
<!DOCTYPE html>

<html>

<head>
```

```html
    <title>{{ title }}</title>
</head>
<body>
    <h1>{{ heading }}</h1>
    <p>{{ content }}</p>
</body>
</html>
```

Modify your Flask application to render the template:

```python
from flask import Flask, render_template

app = Flask(__name__)


@app.route('/')
def home():
    return render_template('index.html', title='Home',
heading='Welcome to My Website', content='This is the home page.')


if __name__ == '__main__':
    app.run(debug=True)
```

4. Handling Forms

Create a form in your index.html **template:**

```html
<!DOCTYPE html>
```

```html
<html>
<head>
    <title>{{ title }}</title>
</head>
<body>
    <h1>{{ heading }}</h1>
    <form action="/submit" method="POST">
        <label for="name">Name:</label>
        <input type="text" id="name" name="name">
        <button type="submit">Submit</button>
    </form>
    <p>{{ content }}</p>
</body>
</html>
```

Update your Flask application to handle form submissions:

```python
from flask import Flask, render_template, request


app = Flask(__name__)


@app.route('/')
def home():
```

```
    return render_template('index.html', title='Home',
heading='Welcome to My Website', content='This is the home page.')


@app.route('/submit', methods=['POST'])

def submit():

    name = request.form['name']

    return f'Hello, {name}!'


if __name__ == '__main__':

    app.run(debug=True)
```

Practical Exercise: To-Do List Application

Let's build a simple to-do list application using Flask.

1. **Set Up the Project**

Create the following directory structure:

```
todo_app/

    app.py

    templates/

        index.html

    static/

        style.css
```

2. **Create the Flask Application**

In app.py, set up the basic Flask application:

```
from flask import Flask, render_template, request, redirect, url_for

app = Flask(__name__)

tasks = []

@app.route('/')
def home():
    return render_template('index.html', tasks=tasks)

@app.route('/add', methods=['POST'])
def add_task():
    task = request.form['task']
    tasks.append(task)
    return redirect(url_for('home'))

if __name__ == '__main__':
    app.run(debug=True)
```

3. Create the HTML Template

In `templates/index.html`, create the HTML template for the to-do list:

```html
<!DOCTYPE html>

<html>

<head>

    <title>To-Do List</title>

    <link rel="stylesheet" type="text/css" href="{{ url_for('static',
filename='style.css') }}">

</head>

<body>

    <h1>To-Do List</h1>

    <form action="/add" method="POST">

        <input type="text" name="task" placeholder="Enter a new task">

        <button type="submit">Add Task</button>

    </form>

    <ul>

        {% for task in tasks %}

        <li>{{ task }}</li>

        {% endfor %}

    </ul>

</body>

</html>
```

4. Add CSS Styling

In `static/style.css`, add some basic styling:

```css
body {
    font-family: Arial, sans-serif;
}


h1 {
    color: #333;
}


form {
    margin-bottom: 20px;
}


input[type="text"] {
    padding: 10px;
    font-size: 16px;
}


button {
    padding: 10px 15px;
    font-size: 16px;
```

```
}


ul {

    list-style-type: none;

    padding: 0;

}


li {

    padding: 10px;

    border-bottom: 1px solid #ccc;

}
```

5. Run the Application

Run your Flask application:

```
python app.py
```

Visit `http://127.0.0.1:5000/` in your web browser to see your to-do list application.

Conclusion

In this chapter, we covered the basics of web development, including HTML, CSS, JavaScript, and how to create a simple web application using Flask. Understanding these foundational technologies will enable you to build dynamic and interactive web applications.

In the next chapter, we will explore more advanced topics in web development, such as working with databases in web applications, user authentication, and deploying your web app to the cloud. Keep practicing, and let's continue your journey to becoming a proficient self-taught developer!

Chapter 9: Advanced Web Development

Introduction

Building on the basics of web development, this chapter delves into more advanced topics, such as integrating databases with web applications, implementing user authentication, and deploying your web app to the cloud. These skills will enable you to create more complex and secure web applications.

Integrating Databases with Flask

To store and manage data in your web applications, you can integrate a database. We'll use SQLite for simplicity, but the concepts apply to other relational databases like MySQL and PostgreSQL.

Setting Up SQLAlchemy

SQLAlchemy is an ORM (Object Relational Mapper) that makes it easier to work with databases in Flask.

1. **Install SQLAlchemy**

```
pip install flask-sqlalchemy
```

2. **Configure Flask to Use SQLAlchemy**

In app.py, set up SQLAlchemy:

```python
from flask import Flask, render_template, request, redirect, url_for

from flask_sqlalchemy import SQLAlchemy


app = Flask(__name__)

app.config['SQLALCHEMY_DATABASE_URI'] = 'sqlite:///tasks.db'

app.config['SQLALCHEMY_TRACK_MODIFICATIONS'] = False

db = SQLAlchemy(app)
```

```python
class Task(db.Model):

    id = db.Column(db.Integer, primary_key=True)

    title = db.Column(db.String(100), nullable=False)

    completed = db.Column(db.Boolean, default=False)


@app.route('/')

def home():

    tasks = Task.query.all()

    return render_template('index.html', tasks=tasks)


@app.route('/add', methods=['POST'])

def add_task():

    task_title = request.form['task']

    new_task = Task(title=task_title)

    db.session.add(new_task)

    db.session.commit()

    return redirect(url_for('home'))


if __name__ == '__main__':

    db.create_all()

    app.run(debug=True)
```

Update Templates

In `index.html`, update the template to display tasks from the database:

```html
<!DOCTYPE html>

<html>

<head>

    <title>To-Do List</title>

    <link rel="stylesheet" type="text/css" href="{{ url_for('static',
filename='style.css') }}">

</head>

<body>

    <h1>To-Do List</h1>

    <form action="/add" method="POST">

        <input type="text" name="task" placeholder="Enter a new task">

        <button type="submit">Add Task</button>

    </form>

    <ul>

        {% for task in tasks %}

        <li>{{ task.title }}</li>

        {% endfor %}

    </ul>

</body>

</html>
```

User Authentication

Implementing user authentication allows you to control access to certain parts of your application. Flask-Login is a library that helps manage user sessions in Flask.

1. **Install Flask-Login**

```
pip install flask-login
```

2. **Set Up User Model**

Update app.py to include user authentication:

```python
from flask import Flask, render_template, request, redirect, url_for, flash

from flask_sqlalchemy import SQLAlchemy

from flask_login import LoginManager, UserMixin, login_user, login_required, logout_user, current_user


app = Flask(__name__)

app.config['SQLALCHEMY_DATABASE_URI'] = 'sqlite:///tasks.db'

app.config['SQLALCHEMY_TRACK_MODIFICATIONS'] = False

app.config['SECRET_KEY'] = 'your_secret_key'

db = SQLAlchemy(app)

login_manager = LoginManager(app)

login_manager.login_view = 'login'


class User(UserMixin, db.Model):

    id = db.Column(db.Integer, primary_key=True)

    username = db.Column(db.String(150), unique=True, nullable=False)
```

```python
        password = db.Column(db.String(150), nullable=False)


class Task(db.Model):

    id = db.Column(db.Integer, primary_key=True)

    title = db.Column(db.String(100), nullable=False)

    completed = db.Column(db.Boolean, default=False)


@login_manager.user_loader

def load_user(user_id):

    return User.query.get(int(user_id))


@app.route('/login', methods=['GET', 'POST'])

def login():

    if request.method == 'POST':

        username = request.form['username']

        password = request.form['password']

        user = User.query.filter_by(username=username).first()

        if user and user.password == password:

            login_user(user)

            return redirect(url_for('home'))

        else:

            flash('Login Unsuccessful. Please check username and
password', 'danger')
```

```python
    return render_template('login.html')


@app.route('/logout')
@login_required
def logout():
    logout_user()
    return redirect(url_for('login'))


@app.route('/')
@login_required
def home():
    tasks = Task.query.all()
    return render_template('index.html', tasks=tasks)


@app.route('/add', methods=['POST'])
@login_required
def add_task():
    task_title = request.form['task']
    new_task = Task(title=task_title)
    db.session.add(new_task)
    db.session.commit()
    return redirect(url_for('home'))
```

```python
if __name__ == '__main__':

    db.create_all()

    app.run(debug=True)
```

3. **Create Login Template**

In `templates/login.html`, create the login template:

```html
<!DOCTYPE html>

<html>

<head>

    <title>Login</title>

</head>

<body>

    <h1>Login</h1>

    <form method="POST">

        <label for="username">Username:</label>

        <input type="text" name="username" id="username" required>

        <label for="password">Password:</label>

        <input type="password" name="password" id="password" required>

        <button type="submit">Login</button>

    </form>

    {% with messages = get_flashed_messages(with_categories=true) %}

    {% if messages %}

        {% for category, message in messages %}
```

```
            <p class="{{ category }}">{{ message }}</p>

        {% endfor %}

    {% endif %}

    {% endwith %}

</body>

</html>
```

Deploying Your Web Application

Deploying your web application makes it accessible to users on the internet. There are various platforms available for deploying web applications, such as Heroku, AWS, and DigitalOcean. We'll use Heroku for this example.

1. **Install Heroku CLI**

Follow the instructions on the Heroku CLI page to install the Heroku CLI.

2. **Log In to Heroku**

```
heroku login
```

3. **Create a Heroku App**

Navigate to your project directory and create a Heroku app:

```
heroku create your-app-name
```

4. **Prepare Your Project for Deployment**

Create a Procfile to specify the command to run your application:

```
web: python app.py
```

Create a `requirements.txt` file with the required dependencies:

```
pip freeze > requirements.txt
```

5. Deploy to Heroku

Initialize a Git repository, add your files, and deploy to Heroku:

```
git init

git add .

git commit -m "Initial commit"

heroku git:remote -a your-app-name

git push heroku master
```

6. Open Your App

Open your deployed application in your browser:

```
heroku open
```

Conclusion

In this chapter, we covered advanced topics in web development, including integrating databases with Flask, implementing user authentication, and deploying your web application to Heroku. These skills will enable you to create more sophisticated and secure web applications.

In the next chapter, we will explore front-end frameworks like React and Vue.js to enhance the user interface and experience of your web applications. Keep practicing, and let's continue your journey to becoming a proficient self-taught developer!

Chapter 10: Enhancing User Interfaces with Front-End Frameworks

Introduction

Front-end frameworks provide a powerful way to build dynamic and interactive user interfaces for web applications. In this chapter, we'll explore two popular front-end frameworks: React and Vue.js. We'll cover the basics of each framework, how to set up your development environment, and how to integrate them with your existing Flask application.

Introduction to React

React is a JavaScript library for building user interfaces. It allows you to create reusable UI components and manage the state of your application efficiently.

Setting Up React

1. **Install Node.js and npm**

Ensure you have Node.js and npm (Node Package Manager) installed. Download and install them from Node.js.

2. **Create a React Application**

Use the `create-react-app` command-line tool to set up a new React project.

```
npx create-react-app my-react-app
cd my-react-app
npm start
```

This command creates a new React application and starts the development server. Open `http://localhost:3000/` in your browser to see the default React application.

React Components

React applications are built using components. Each component represents a part of the user interface.

1. **Create a New Component**

Create a new file named `TaskList.js` in the `src` directory.

```
import React from 'react';
```

```
const TaskList = ({ tasks }) => {
    return (
        <div>
            <h2>Task List</h2>
            <ul>
                {tasks.map(task => (
                    <li key={task.id}>{task.title}</li>
                ))}
            </ul>
        </div>
    );
};

export default TaskList;
```

2. Use the Component in Your Application

Update src/App.js to use the TaskList component.

```
import React, { useState, useEffect } from 'react';
import TaskList from './TaskList';

const App = () => {
    const [tasks, setTasks] = useState([]);

    useEffect(() => {
        fetch('/api/tasks')
            .then(response => response.json())
            .then(data => setTasks(data));
    }, []);

    return (
        <div className="App">
            <h1>To-Do List</h1>
            <TaskList tasks={tasks} />
        </div>
    );
};
```

```
export default App;
```

3. Integrate with Flask

Update your Flask application to serve the React app. Install `flask-cors` to handle cross-origin requests.

```
pip install flask-cors
```

In `app.py`, configure CORS and create an endpoint to serve tasks.

```python
from flask import Flask, jsonify
from flask_cors import CORS

app = Flask(__name__)
CORS(app)

@app.route('/api/tasks', methods=['GET'])
def get_tasks():
    tasks = Task.query.all()
    tasks_list = [{'id': task.id, 'title': task.title, 'completed':
task.completed} for task in tasks]
    return jsonify(tasks_list)

if __name__ == '__main__':
    app.run(debug=True)
```

Introduction to Vue.js

Vue.js is another popular front-end framework for building user interfaces. It is known for its simplicity and flexibility.

Setting Up Vue.js

1. Install Vue CLI

Install Vue CLI using npm.

```
npm install -g @vue/cli
```

2. Create a Vue Application

Create a new Vue project using Vue CLI.

```
vue create my-vue-app
cd my-vue-app
npm run serve
```

This command sets up a new Vue application and starts the development server. Open `http://localhost:8080/` in your browser to see the default Vue application.

Vue Components

Vue applications are built using components. Each component encapsulates its own structure, style, and behavior.

1. Create a New Component

Create a new file named `TaskList.vue` in the `src/components` directory.

```
<template>
  <div>
    <h2>Task List</h2>
    <ul>
      <li v-for="task in tasks" :key="task.id">{{ task.title }}</li>
    </ul>
  </div>
</template>
```

```
<script>
export default {
  props: ['tasks']
};
</script>

<style scoped>
/* Add component-specific styles here */
</style>
```

2. **Use the Component in Your Application**

Update src/App.vue to use the TaskList component.

```
<template>
  <div id="app">
    <h1>To-Do List</h1>
    <TaskList :tasks="tasks" />
  </div>
</template>

<script>
import TaskList from './components/TaskList.vue';

export default {
  name: 'App',
  components: {
    TaskList
  },
  data() {
    return {
      tasks: []
    };
  },
  created() {
    fetch('/api/tasks')
      .then(response => response.json())
      .then(data => {
        this.tasks = data;
```

```
      });
  }
};
</script>

<style>
/* Add global styles here */
</style>
```

3. **Integrate with Flask**

Ensure your Flask application is configured to handle cross-origin requests, as shown in the previous React example.

Deploying Your Front-End Application

Deploying a front-end application involves building the static files and serving them through your Flask application.

1. **Build the Front-End Application**

For React:

```
npm run build
```

For Vue.js:

```
npm run build
```

2. **Serve Static Files with Flask**

Update app.py to serve the static files.

```
from flask import Flask, send_from_directory

app = Flask(__name__, static_folder='build')

@app.route('/')
def serve():
    return send_from_directory(app.static_folder, 'index.html')
```

```python
@app.route('/<path:path>')
def static_proxy(path):
    return send_from_directory(app.static_folder, path)

@app.route('/api/tasks', methods=['GET'])
def get_tasks():
    tasks = Task.query.all()
    tasks_list = [{'id': task.id, 'title': task.title, 'completed':
task.completed} for task in tasks]
    return jsonify(tasks_list)

if __name__ == '__main__':
    app.run(debug=True)
```

Conclusion

In this chapter, we explored two popular front-end frameworks, React and Vue.js, and how to set up and integrate them with your Flask application. These frameworks enable you to build dynamic and interactive user interfaces, enhancing the overall user experience of your web applications.

In the next chapter, we will delve into advanced topics such as state management, routing in single-page applications, and best practices for front-end development. Keep practicing, and let's continue your journey to becoming a proficient self-taught developer!

Chapter 11: Advanced Front-End Development

Introduction

Building on the basics of React and Vue.js, this chapter will cover more advanced topics in front-end development. We will explore state management, routing in single-page applications, and best practices for maintaining and optimizing front-end code.

State Management

Managing the state of your application is crucial for creating responsive and dynamic user interfaces. Both React and Vue.js have libraries and tools designed for state management.

State Management in React

React uses a context API and state management libraries like Redux for handling application state.

1. **Using React Context API**

The Context API is a way to pass data through the component tree without having to pass props down manually at every level.

```
import React, { createContext, useState, useContext } from 'react';

// Create a Context
const TaskContext = createContext();

// Create a provider component
const TaskProvider = ({ children }) => {
    const [tasks, setTasks] = useState([]);

    return (
        <TaskContext.Provider value={{ tasks, setTasks }}>
            {children}
        </TaskContext.Provider>
    );
};

// Custom hook to use the TaskContext
const useTasks = () => {
    return useContext(TaskContext);
```

```
    };

    const TaskList = () => {
        const { tasks } = useTasks();

        return (
            <div>
                <h2>Task List</h2>
                <ul>
                    {tasks.map(task => (
                        <li key={task.id}>{task.title}</li>
                    ))}
                </ul>
            </div>
        );
    };

    const App = () => {
        const { setTasks } = useTasks();

        useEffect(() => {
            fetch('/api/tasks')
                .then(response => response.json())
                .then(data => setTasks(data));
        }, []);

        return (
            <div className="App">
                <h1>To-Do List</h1>
                <TaskList />
            </div>
        );
    };

    // Wrap your application in the provider
    export default () => (
        <TaskProvider>
            <App />
```

```
    </TaskProvider>
);
```

2. Using Redux

Redux is a predictable state container for JavaScript apps.

```
npm install redux react-redux
```

Set up Redux in your React application:

```
import { createStore } from 'redux';
import { Provider, useDispatch, useSelector } from 'react-redux';

const initialState = {
    tasks: []
};

const reducer = (state = initialState, action) => {
    switch (action.type) {
        case 'SET_TASKS':
            return { ...state, tasks: action.tasks };
        default:
            return state;
    }
};

const store = createStore(reducer);

const App = () => {
    const dispatch = useDispatch();
    const tasks = useSelector(state => state.tasks);

    useEffect(() => {
        fetch('/api/tasks')
            .then(response => response.json())
            .then(data => dispatch({ type: 'SET_TASKS', tasks: data
}));
    }, [dispatch]);
```

```
        return (
            <div className="App">
                <h1>To-Do List</h1>
                <ul>
                    {tasks.map(task => (
                        <li key={task.id}>{task.title}</li>
                    ))}
                </ul>
            </div>
        );
};

export default () => (
    <Provider store={store}>
        <App />
    </Provider>
);
```

State Management in Vue.js

Vue.js uses Vuex for state management.

1. **Installing Vuex**

```
npm install vuex
```

2. **Setting Up Vuex Store**

Create a store.js file:

```
import Vue from 'vue';
import Vuex from 'vuex';

Vue.use(Vuex);

export default new Vuex.Store({
    state: {
        tasks: []
```

```
    },
    mutations: {
        setTasks(state, tasks) {
            state.tasks = tasks;
        }
    },
    actions: {
        fetchTasks({ commit }) {
            fetch('/api/tasks')
                .then(response => response.json())
                .then(data => commit('setTasks', data));
        }
    },
    getters: {
        tasks: state => state.tasks
    }
});
```

3. Using Vuex in Your Application

In main.js, import and use the store:

```
import Vue from 'vue';
import App from './App.vue';
import store from './store';

new Vue({
    store,
    render: h => h(App)
}).$mount('#app');
```

In your components:

```
<template>
  <div id="app">
    <h1>To-Do List</h1>
    <ul>
      <li v-for="task in tasks" :key="task.id">{{ task.title }}</li>
```

```
      </ul>
    </div>
</template>

<script>
export default {
  computed: {
    tasks() {
      return this.$store.getters.tasks;
    }
  },
  created() {
    this.$store.dispatch('fetchTasks');
  }
};
</script>
```

Routing in Single-Page Applications

Routing allows you to navigate between different views or pages in your application without reloading the page.

Routing in React

React Router is the standard library for routing in React applications.

1. **Installing React Router**

```
npm install react-router-dom
```

2. **Setting Up Routes**

```
import { BrowserRouter as Router, Route, Switch, Link } from
'react-router-dom';

const Home = () => <h2>Home</h2>;
const About = () => <h2>About</h2>;

const App = () => (
    <Router>
```

```
        <div>
            <nav>
                <ul>
                    <li><Link to="/">Home</Link></li>
                    <li><Link to="/about">About</Link></li>
                </ul>
            </nav>

            <Switch>
                <Route path="/about">
                    <About />
                </Route>
                <Route path="/">
                    <Home />
                </Route>
            </Switch>
        </div>
    </Router>
);

export default App;
```

Routing in Vue.js

Vue Router is the official router for Vue.js.

1. **Installing Vue Router**

```
npm install vue-router
```

2. **Setting Up Routes**

Create a `router.js` file:

```
import Vue from 'vue';
import Router from 'vue-router';
import Home from './components/Home.vue';
import About from './components/About.vue';
```

```
Vue.use(Router);

export default new Router({
    routes: [
        { path: '/', component: Home },
        { path: '/about', component: About }
    ]
});
```

3. Using the Router in Your Application

In main.js, import and use the router:

```
import Vue from 'vue';
import App from './App.vue';
import router from './router';

new Vue({
    router,
    render: h => h(App)
}).$mount('#app');
```

In your components:

```
<template>
  <div id="app">
    <nav>
      <router-link to="/">Home</router-link>
      <router-link to="/about">About</router-link>
    </nav>
    <router-view></router-view>
  </div>
</template>

<script>
export default {
  name: 'App'
};
```

```
</script>
```

Best Practices for Front-End Development

1. **Code Organization**
   - Structure your project into meaningful directories.
   - Separate components, services, and utilities.
2. **Reusable Components**
   - Create reusable components to avoid code duplication.
   - Use props and slots (Vue) or children (React) for flexibility.
3. **State Management**
   - Use context or state management libraries for handling global state.
   - Keep components stateless whenever possible.
4. **Performance Optimization**
   - Use code splitting and lazy loading to reduce initial load times.
   - Optimize images and assets.
   - Avoid unnecessary re-renders.
5. **Testing**
   - Write unit tests for components.
   - Use end-to-end testing frameworks like Cypress or Selenium.
6. **Version Control**
   - Use version control systems like Git.
   - Follow best practices for commit messages and branching strategies.

Conclusion

In this chapter, we covered advanced topics in front-end development, including state management with React and Vue.js, routing in single-page applications, and best practices for maintaining and optimizing front-end code. These skills will help you build robust, maintainable, and high-performance web applications.

In the next chapter, we will explore mobile app development, including how to build cross-platform mobile applications using frameworks like React Native and Flutter. Keep practicing, and let's continue your journey to becoming a proficient self-taught developer!

Chapter 12: Cross-Platform Mobile App Development

Introduction

Mobile app development allows you to reach users on their smartphones and tablets, creating a more direct and engaging user experience. In this chapter, we will explore the basics of cross-platform mobile app development using React Native and Flutter. These frameworks enable you to build mobile applications for both iOS and Android using a single codebase.

Introduction to React Native

React Native is a popular framework for building mobile applications using JavaScript and React. It allows you to use the same design principles and components as React while providing access to native mobile features.

Setting Up React Native

1. **Install Node.js and npm**

Ensure you have Node.js and npm (Node Package Manager) installed. Download and install them from Node.js.

2. **Install Expo CLI**

Expo CLI is a tool for developing React Native apps quickly.

```
npm install -g expo-cli
```

3. **Create a New React Native Project**

Use Expo CLI to create a new project:

```
expo init MyReactNativeApp
cd MyReactNativeApp
expo start
```

This command sets up a new React Native application and starts the development server. Follow the instructions to open the app on your device using the Expo Go app.

Building a Simple React Native App

1. **Create a Basic Component**

Open `App.js` and modify it to create a simple component:

```javascript
import React, { useState } from 'react';
import { StyleSheet, Text, View, TextInput, Button, FlatList } from
'react-native';

export default function App() {
    const [task, setTask] = useState('');
    const [tasks, setTasks] = useState([]);

    const addTask = () => {
        setTasks([...tasks, { key: Math.random().toString(), value:
task }]);
        setTask('');
    };

    return (
        <View style={styles.container}>
            <Text style={styles.title}>To-Do List</Text>
            <TextInput
                style={styles.input}
                placeholder="Enter a new task"
                value={task}
                onChangeText={setTask}
            />
            <Button title="Add Task" onPress={addTask} />
            <FlatList
                data={tasks}
                renderItem={({ item }) => <Text
style={styles.task}>{item.value}</Text>}
            />
        </View>
    );
}

const styles = StyleSheet.create({
    container: {
        flex: 1,
        backgroundColor: '#fff',
```

```
            alignItems: 'center',
            justifyContent: 'center',
            padding: 20,
        },
        title: {
            fontSize: 24,
            fontWeight: 'bold',
        },
        input: {
            height: 40,
            borderColor: 'gray',
            borderWidth: 1,
            marginBottom: 10,
            paddingHorizontal: 10,
            width: '100%',
        },
        task: {
            padding: 10,
            fontSize: 18,
            borderBottomColor: 'gray',
            borderBottomWidth: 1,
            width: '100%',
        },
});
```

2. **Run the App**

Run your app using the Expo CLI:

```
expo start
```

Use the Expo Go app on your device to scan the QR code and view the app.

Introduction to Flutter

Flutter is a UI toolkit from Google for building natively compiled applications for mobile, web, and desktop from a single codebase. It uses the Dart programming language.

Setting Up Flutter

1. **Install Flutter**

Download and install Flutter from the official Flutter website.

2. **Create a New Flutter Project**

Use the Flutter CLI to create a new project:

```
flutter create my_flutter_app
cd my_flutter_app
flutter run
```

This command sets up a new Flutter application and runs it on the connected device or emulator.

Building a Simple Flutter App

1. **Create a Basic Component**

Open lib/main.dart and modify it to create a simple component:

```
import 'package:flutter/material.dart';

void main() => runApp(MyApp());

class MyApp extends StatelessWidget {
  @override
  Widget build(BuildContext context) {
    return MaterialApp(
      title: 'To-Do List',
      theme: ThemeData(
        primarySwatch: Colors.blue,
      ),
      home: ToDoList(),
    );
  }
}

class ToDoList extends StatefulWidget {
  @override
  _ToDoListState createState() => _ToDoListState();
```

```dart
}

class _ToDoListState extends State<ToDoList> {
  final List<String> _tasks = [];
  final TextEditingController _controller = TextEditingController();

  void _addTask() {
    setState(() {
      _tasks.add(_controller.text);
      _controller.clear();
    });
  }

  @override
  Widget build(BuildContext context) {
    return Scaffold(
      appBar: AppBar(
        title: Text('To-Do List'),
      ),
      body: Column(
        children: <Widget>[
          Padding(
            padding: const EdgeInsets.all(16.0),
            child: TextField(
              controller: _controller,
              decoration: InputDecoration(labelText: 'Enter a new
task'),
            ),
          ),
          ElevatedButton(
            onPressed: _addTask,
            child: Text('Add Task'),
          ),
          Expanded(
            child: ListView.builder(
              itemCount: _tasks.length,
              itemBuilder: (ctx, index) {
                return ListTile(
```

```
                    title: Text(_tasks[index]),
                );
            },
        ),
    ),
    ],
    ),
    );
  }
}
```

2. **Run the App**

Run your app using the Flutter CLI:

```
flutter run
```

This will launch the app on your connected device or emulator.

Comparing React Native and Flutter

Development Experience

- **React Native**: Leverages existing knowledge of JavaScript and React. Uses the vast ecosystem of npm packages.
- **Flutter**: Uses Dart, which may require learning a new language. Provides a comprehensive set of widgets and tools out of the box.

Performance

- **React Native**: Good performance with a bridge to native modules, but may require optimization for complex apps.
- **Flutter**: Excellent performance with a compiled binary and direct access to native components.

Community and Ecosystem

- **React Native**: Large community and mature ecosystem with many third-party libraries.
- **Flutter**: Growing community with strong support from Google and an increasing number of third-party packages.

Best Practices for Mobile App Development

1. **Code Organization**
   - Keep your code modular and organized.
   - Separate business logic from UI components.
2. **State Management**
   - Use state management libraries (e.g., Redux for React Native, Provider for Flutter) to handle complex state.
   - Keep the state as minimal as possible and derive data when needed.
3. **Navigation**
   - Use navigation libraries (e.g., React Navigation for React Native, Navigator for Flutter) for managing app navigation.
   - Plan your navigation structure and routes.
4. **Performance Optimization**
   - Optimize images and assets.
   - Avoid unnecessary re-renders and rebuilds.
   - Use profiling tools to identify and fix performance bottlenecks.
5. **Testing**
   - Write unit tests for your components and business logic.
   - Use integration tests to verify the app's functionality.
6. **User Experience**
   - Follow platform-specific design guidelines (Material Design for Android, Human Interface Guidelines for iOS).
   - Ensure your app is responsive and handles different screen sizes.

Conclusion

In this chapter, we explored cross-platform mobile app development using React Native and Flutter. Both frameworks allow you to build powerful mobile applications for iOS and Android with a single codebase. By following best practices and leveraging the strengths of each framework, you can create high-quality, performant, and user-friendly mobile apps.

In the next chapter, we will dive into cloud computing and explore how to leverage cloud services to enhance your applications. Keep practicing, and let's continue your journey to becoming a proficient self-taught developer!

Chapter 13: Leveraging Cloud Computing

Introduction

Cloud computing has revolutionized the way applications are developed, deployed, and managed. By leveraging cloud services, you can enhance the scalability, availability, and performance of your applications. In this chapter, we will explore the basics of cloud computing, popular cloud service providers, and how to use cloud services to improve your applications.

Understanding Cloud Computing

Cloud computing provides on-demand access to computing resources over the internet. These resources include servers, storage, databases, networking, software, and more. Cloud computing offers several key benefits:

1. **Scalability**: Easily scale resources up or down based on demand.
2. **Cost Efficiency**: Pay only for the resources you use.
3. **Reliability**: Benefit from high availability and disaster recovery solutions.
4. **Flexibility**: Access a wide range of services and tools to build and deploy applications.

Popular Cloud Service Providers

Several cloud service providers offer a variety of services to meet different needs. The most popular providers are:

1. **Amazon Web Services (AWS)**: A comprehensive cloud platform offering a wide range of services, including computing, storage, databases, machine learning, and more.
2. **Microsoft Azure**: A cloud platform providing a broad set of services, including virtual machines, databases, AI, and DevOps tools.
3. **Google Cloud Platform (GCP)**: A suite of cloud services, including computing, data storage, machine learning, and data analytics.

Setting Up Your Cloud Environment

Amazon Web Services (AWS)

1. **Create an AWS Account**
   Sign up for an AWS account at AWS.

Install AWS CLI
The AWS Command Line Interface (CLI) allows you to manage AWS services from your terminal.
```
pip install awscli
```

2.

Configure AWS CLI
```
aws configure
```

3. Follow the prompts to enter your AWS Access Key, Secret Access Key, region, and output format.

Creating an EC2 Instance
Launch an EC2 instance (a virtual server) using the AWS Management Console or CLI.
```
aws ec2 run-instances --image-id ami-0c55b159cbfafe1f0 --instance-type
t2.micro --key-name MyKeyPair --security-group-ids sg-xxxxxxxx
--subnet-id subnet-xxxxxxxx
```

4.

Microsoft Azure

1. **Create an Azure Account**
   Sign up for an Azure account at <u>Azure</u>.

Install Azure CLI
The Azure Command-Line Interface (CLI) allows you to manage Azure resources from your terminal.
```
curl -sL https://aka.ms/InstallAzureCLIDeb | sudo bash
```

2.

Login to Azure
```
az login
```

3.

Creating a Virtual Machine
```
az vm create --resource-group myResourceGroup --name myVM --image
UbuntuLTS --admin-username azureuser --generate-ssh-keys
```

4.

Google Cloud Platform (GCP)

1. **Create a Google Cloud Account**
   Sign up for a Google Cloud account at <u>GCP</u>.

Install Google Cloud SDK
The Google Cloud SDK allows you to manage GCP resources from your terminal.

```
curl https://sdk.cloud.google.com | bash
```

```
exec -l $SHELL
```

```
gcloud init
```

2.

Creating a Compute Engine Instance

```
gcloud compute instances create my-instance --zone=us-central1-a
--machine-type=e2-micro --image-project=debian-cloud
--image-family=debian-10
```

3.

Deploying Applications to the Cloud

Deploying a Flask Application to AWS Elastic Beanstalk

Install Elastic Beanstalk CLI

```
pip install awsebcli
```

1.

Initialize Elastic Beanstalk

```
eb init -p python-3.7 my-flask-app
```

2.

Create an Elastic Beanstalk Environment

```
eb create my-flask-env
```

3.

Deploy the Application

```
eb deploy
```

4.

Open the Application

```
eb open
```

5.

Deploying a Node.js Application to Azure App Service

Create an App Service Plan

```
az appservice plan create --name myAppServicePlan --resource-group
myResourceGroup --sku FREE
```

1.

Create a Web App

```
az webapp create --resource-group myResourceGroup --plan
myAppServicePlan --name my-web-app --runtime "NODE|12-lts"
```

2.

Deploy the Application
Use the Azure CLI to deploy your application:

```
az webapp up --name my-web-app --resource-group myResourceGroup
```

3.

Open the Application
Open your web app in the browser:

```
az webapp browse --name my-web-app --resource-group myResourceGroup
```

4.

Deploying a Python Application to Google App Engine

Create an App Engine Application

```
gcloud app create --project=my-project
```

1.

Deploy the Application
Create an `app.yaml` file with your application configuration:

```
runtime: python37
```

Deploy your application:

```
gcloud app deploy
```

2.

Open the Application
Open your application in the browser:

```
gcloud app browse
```

3.

Best Practices for Cloud Development

1. **Security**
   - Use strong authentication and access controls.
   - Encrypt data at rest and in transit.
   - Regularly update and patch your systems.
2. **Cost Management**
   - Monitor and optimize your resource usage.
   - Use cost management tools provided by your cloud provider.
   - Set up billing alerts to avoid unexpected charges.
3. **Scalability**
   - Design your application to scale horizontally.
   - Use auto-scaling features to handle varying loads.
   - Optimize your database queries and indexing.
4. **Backup and Recovery**
   - Implement regular backups of your data.
   - Test your disaster recovery plan.
   - Use version control and CI/CD pipelines for code deployment.

Conclusion

In this chapter, we explored the basics of cloud computing and how to leverage cloud services to enhance your applications. By using cloud services from providers like AWS, Azure, and GCP, you can improve the scalability, availability, and performance of your applications. Following best practices for cloud development will help you build secure, cost-efficient, and reliable solutions.

In the next chapter, we will delve into DevOps practices, including continuous integration and continuous deployment (CI/CD), to streamline your development and deployment processes. Keep practicing, and let's continue your journey to becoming a proficient self-taught developer!

Chapter 14: DevOps and Continuous Integration/Continuous Deployment (CI/CD)

Introduction

DevOps is a set of practices that combines software development (Dev) and IT operations (Ops) to shorten the development lifecycle and deliver high-quality software continuously. Continuous Integration (CI) and Continuous Deployment (CD) are key components of DevOps that automate the process of integrating code changes and deploying applications. In this chapter, we will explore the fundamentals of DevOps, CI/CD, and how to implement these practices using popular tools.

Understanding DevOps

DevOps aims to improve collaboration between development and operations teams, automate processes, and enhance the reliability and security of software systems. The main goals of DevOps include:

1. **Continuous Integration**: Frequently integrating code changes into a shared repository, followed by automated builds and tests.
2. **Continuous Deployment**: Automatically deploying code changes to production environments after passing all tests.
3. **Infrastructure as Code (IaC)**: Managing and provisioning infrastructure using code and automation tools.
4. **Monitoring and Logging**: Continuously monitoring applications and infrastructure to ensure performance and reliability.

Continuous Integration (CI)

CI involves automatically integrating code changes from multiple developers into a shared repository and running automated tests to detect issues early.

Setting Up a CI Pipeline with GitHub Actions

GitHub Actions is a CI/CD tool integrated with GitHub that allows you to automate workflows.

1. **Create a GitHub Repository**
   Create a new repository on GitHub for your project.

Add a CI Workflow
In your repository, create a `.github/workflows/ci.yml` file with the following content:

```
name: CI
```

```yaml
on:
  push:
    branches:
      - main
  pull_request:
    branches:
      - main

jobs:
  build:
    runs-on: ubuntu-latest

    steps:
    - uses: actions/checkout@v2
    - name: Set up Python
      uses: actions/setup-python@v2
      with:
        python-version: '3.8'
    - name: Install dependencies
      run: |
        python -m pip install --upgrade pip
        pip install -r requirements.txt
    - name: Run tests
```

```
    run: |

      pytest
```

2. This workflow runs on every push to the main branch and on pull requests. It sets up
   Python, installs dependencies, and runs tests using `pytest`.

Commit and Push Changes
Commit and push your changes to trigger the CI workflow:

```
git add .

git commit -m "Set up CI with GitHub Actions"

git push origin main
```

3.
4. **View CI Results**
   Open your GitHub repository and navigate to the "Actions" tab to view the results of your
   CI workflow.

Continuous Deployment (CD)

CD involves automatically deploying code changes to production environments after they pass
all tests. This ensures that new features and bug fixes are delivered quickly and reliably.

Setting Up a CD Pipeline with GitHub Actions

Extend your CI workflow to include deployment steps.

Add Deployment Steps
Update your `.github/workflows/ci.yml` file to include deployment steps:

```
name: CI/CD


on:

  push:

    branches:

      - main

  pull_request:
```

```yaml
    branches:
      - main

jobs:
  build:
    runs-on: ubuntu-latest

    steps:
    - uses: actions/checkout@v2
    - name: Set up Python
      uses: actions/setup-python@v2
      with:
        python-version: '3.8'
    - name: Install dependencies
      run: |
        python -m pip install --upgrade pip
        pip install -r requirements.txt
    - name: Run tests
      run: |
        pytest
    - name: Deploy to Heroku
      env:
        HEROKU_API_KEY: ${{ secrets.HEROKU_API_KEY }}
```

```
      run: |

        git remote add heroku
https://git.heroku.com/your-heroku-app.git

          git push heroku main
```

1. This workflow includes a deployment step to Heroku. You need to add your Heroku API key as a secret in your GitHub repository settings.
2. **Add Heroku API Key to GitHub Secrets**
   Go to your GitHub repository settings, navigate to "Secrets," and add a new secret named `HEROKU_API_KEY` with your Heroku API key.

Commit and Push Changes
Commit and push your changes to trigger the CI/CD workflow:
```
git add .

git commit -m "Set up CD with GitHub Actions"

git push origin main
```

3.
4. **View Deployment Results**
   Open your GitHub repository and navigate to the "Actions" tab to view the results of your CI/CD workflow.

Infrastructure as Code (IaC)

IaC involves managing and provisioning infrastructure using code and automation tools. This allows you to version control your infrastructure and automate the provisioning process.

Using Terraform for IaC

Terraform is an open-source IaC tool that allows you to define and provision infrastructure using a declarative configuration language.

1. **Install Terraform**
   Follow the installation instructions on the Terraform website.

Create a Terraform Configuration
Create a `main.tf` file with the following content:
```
provider "aws" {

  region = "us-west-2"
```

```
}
```

```
resource "aws_instance" "example" {

  ami            = "ami-0c55b159cbfafe1f0"

  instance_type = "t2.micro"


  tags = {

    Name = "example-instance"

  }

}
```

2. This configuration defines an AWS EC2 instance.

Initialize Terraform
Initialize Terraform to download the necessary plugins:
```
terraform init
```

3.

Apply the Configuration
Apply the configuration to provision the infrastructure:
```
terraform apply
```

4.

Manage Infrastructure Changes
Use Terraform to manage and apply changes to your infrastructure. For example, to change the instance type:
```
resource "aws_instance" "example" {

  ami            = "ami-0c55b159cbfafe1f0"

  instance_type = "t2.small"
```

```
  tags = {

    Name = "example-instance"

  }

}
```

Apply the changes:
```
terraform apply
```

    5.

Monitoring and Logging

Monitoring and logging are essential for ensuring the performance and reliability of your applications and infrastructure.

Using Prometheus and Grafana

Prometheus is an open-source monitoring and alerting toolkit, and Grafana is an open-source platform for monitoring and observability.

    1. **Install Prometheus**
       Follow the installation instructions on the Prometheus website.

Configure Prometheus

Create a `prometheus.yml` configuration file:
```
global:

  scrape_interval: 15s


scrape_configs:

  - job_name: 'prometheus'

    static_configs:

      - targets: ['localhost:9090']
```

    2.

Start Prometheus

Start Prometheus using the configuration file:

```
./prometheus --config.file=prometheus.yml
```

3.
4. **Install Grafana**
   Follow the installation instructions on the Grafana website.
5. **Configure Grafana**
   Add Prometheus as a data source in Grafana and create dashboards to visualize metrics.

Best Practices for DevOps

1. **Automate Everything**
   - Automate builds, tests, deployments, and infrastructure provisioning.
   - Use CI/CD pipelines to ensure code changes are integrated and deployed continuously.
2. **Version Control**
   - Use version control for both code and infrastructure.
   - Maintain a clean and organized repository structure.
3. **Monitoring and Logging**
   - Implement comprehensive monitoring and logging for applications and infrastructure.
   - Set up alerts to detect and respond to issues promptly.
4. **Security**
   - Implement security best practices, such as encryption, access controls, and regular security audits.
   - Use tools and services to scan for vulnerabilities and ensure compliance.
5. **Collaboration**
   - Foster a culture of collaboration between development and operations teams.
   - Use collaboration tools to streamline communication and project management.

Conclusion

In this chapter, we explored the fundamentals of DevOps and how to implement Continuous Integration (CI) and Continuous Deployment (CD) using GitHub Actions. We also covered Infrastructure as Code (IaC) with Terraform and the importance of monitoring and logging. By adopting DevOps practices, you can streamline your development and deployment processes, improve collaboration, and ensure the reliability and security of your applications.

In the next chapter, we will delve into machine learning and artificial intelligence, exploring how to build and deploy intelligent applications. Keep practicing, and let's continue your journey to becoming a proficient self-taught developer!

Chapter 15: Introduction to Machine Learning and Artificial Intelligence

Introduction

Machine Learning (ML) and Artificial Intelligence (AI) are transforming industries by enabling computers to learn from data and make intelligent decisions. In this chapter, we will explore the basics of machine learning, different types of machine learning algorithms, and how to build and deploy ML models using popular frameworks such as Scikit-Learn, TensorFlow, and PyTorch.

Understanding Machine Learning

Machine learning is a subset of AI that focuses on developing algorithms that allow computers to learn from and make predictions based on data. The key components of machine learning include:

1. **Data**: The foundation of any machine learning model. High-quality data is crucial for training effective models.
2. **Features**: Attributes or properties of the data used to make predictions.
3. **Model**: The mathematical representation of the learning process.
4. **Training**: The process of teaching the model to make accurate predictions by exposing it to data.
5. **Evaluation**: Assessing the performance of the model using metrics such as accuracy, precision, and recall.

Types of Machine Learning

1. **Supervised Learning**: The model is trained on labeled data, meaning that each training example is paired with an output label. Common algorithms include linear regression, logistic regression, decision trees, and support vector machines.
2. **Unsupervised Learning**: The model is trained on unlabeled data, and the goal is to identify patterns or structures in the data. Common algorithms include clustering (e.g., K-means) and dimensionality reduction (e.g., PCA).
3. **Reinforcement Learning**: The model learns by interacting with an environment and receiving feedback in the form of rewards or penalties. This approach is often used in robotics, gaming, and autonomous systems.

Building Machine Learning Models

Setting Up Your Environment
Install Python and Jupyter Notebook
Ensure you have Python installed. Install Jupyter Notebook using pip:

```
pip install jupyter
```

1.

Install Machine Learning Libraries
Install popular ML libraries such as Scikit-Learn, TensorFlow, and PyTorch:

```
pip install scikit-learn tensorflow torch
```

2.

Building a Simple Model with Scikit-Learn

Scikit-Learn is a powerful and easy-to-use library for machine learning in Python.

Import Libraries and Load Data

```
import numpy as np
import pandas as pd
from sklearn.model_selection import train_test_split
from sklearn.linear_model import LinearRegression
from sklearn.metrics import mean_squared_error

# Load data
data = pd.read_csv('data/housing.csv')
X = data[['feature1', 'feature2', 'feature3']]
y = data['target']
```

1.

Split Data into Training and Testing Sets

```
X_train, X_test, y_train, y_test = train_test_split(X, y,
test_size=0.2, random_state=42)
```

2.

Train a Linear Regression Model

```
model = LinearRegression()
model.fit(X_train, y_train)
```

3.

Evaluate the Model

```
y_pred = model.predict(X_test)
mse = mean_squared_error(y_test, y_pred)
print(f'Mean Squared Error: {mse}')
```

4.

Building a Neural Network with TensorFlow

TensorFlow is an open-source library for numerical computation and machine learning.

Import Libraries and Load Data

```python
import tensorflow as tf
from tensorflow.keras.models import Sequential
from tensorflow.keras.layers import Dense
from sklearn.model_selection import train_test_split
from sklearn.preprocessing import StandardScaler

# Load data
data = pd.read_csv('data/housing.csv')
X = data[['feature1', 'feature2', 'feature3']]
y = data['target']
```

1.

Preprocess Data

```python
X_train, X_test, y_train, y_test = train_test_split(X, y,
test_size=0.2, random_state=42)
scaler = StandardScaler()
X_train = scaler.fit_transform(X_train)
X_test = scaler.transform(X_test)
```

2.

Build and Train the Model

```python
model = Sequential([
    Dense(64, activation='relu', input_shape=(X_train.shape[1],)),
    Dense(64, activation='relu'),
    Dense(1)
])

model.compile(optimizer='adam', loss='mse')
model.fit(X_train, y_train, epochs=10, batch_size=32,
validation_split=0.2)
```

3.

Evaluate the Model

```python
loss = model.evaluate(X_test, y_test)
```

```
print(f'Test Loss: {loss}')
```

4.

Building a Neural Network with PyTorch

PyTorch is an open-source machine learning library for Python based on Torch.

Import Libraries and Load Data
```
import torch
import torch.nn as nn
import torch.optim as optim
from sklearn.model_selection import train_test_split
from sklearn.preprocessing import StandardScaler

# Load data
data = pd.read_csv('data/housing.csv')
X = data[['feature1', 'feature2', 'feature3']]
y = data['target'].values
```

1.

Preprocess Data
```
X_train, X_test, y_train, y_test = train_test_split(X, y,
test_size=0.2, random_state=42)
scaler = StandardScaler()
X_train = scaler.fit_transform(X_train)
X_test = scaler.transform(X_test)
```

2.

Convert Data to Tensors
```
X_train = torch.tensor(X_train, dtype=torch.float32)
X_test = torch.tensor(X_test, dtype=torch.float32)
y_train = torch.tensor(y_train, dtype=torch.float32).view(-1, 1)
y_test = torch.tensor(y_test, dtype=torch.float32).view(-1, 1)
```

3.

Build and Train the Model
```
class NeuralNetwork(nn.Module):
    def __init__(self):
        super(NeuralNetwork, self).__init__()
```

```python
        self.layer1 = nn.Linear(X_train.shape[1], 64)
        self.layer2 = nn.Linear(64, 64)
        self.output = nn.Linear(64, 1)

    def forward(self, x):
        x = torch.relu(self.layer1(x))
        x = torch.relu(self.layer2(x))
        x = self.output(x)
        return x

model = NeuralNetwork()
criterion = nn.MSELoss()
optimizer = optim.Adam(model.parameters(), lr=0.001)

for epoch in range(10):
    model.train()
    optimizer.zero_grad()
    outputs = model(X_train)
    loss = criterion(outputs, y_train)
    loss.backward()
    optimizer.step()
    print(f'Epoch {epoch+1}, Loss: {loss.item()}')
```

4.

Evaluate the Model
```python
model.eval()
with torch.no_grad():
    predictions = model(X_test)
    test_loss = criterion(predictions, y_test)
    print(f'Test Loss: {test_loss.item()}')
```

5.

Deploying Machine Learning Models

Deploying machine learning models allows you to use them in production environments to make predictions and provide intelligent features in your applications.

Deploying with Flask

You can use Flask to deploy your machine learning models as web services.

Create a Flask Application

```python
from flask import Flask, request, jsonify
import joblib
import numpy as np

app = Flask(__name__)

# Load the trained model
model = joblib.load('model.pkl')

@app.route('/predict', methods=['POST'])
def predict():
    data = request.get_json()
    features = np.array(data['features']).reshape(1, -1)
    prediction = model.predict(features)
    return jsonify({'prediction': prediction[0]})

if __name__ == '__main__':
    app.run(debug=True)
```

1.

Save the Trained Model

```python
from sklearn.externals import joblib

# Train your model (as shown in the previous sections)
joblib.dump(model, 'model.pkl')
```

2.

Run the Flask Application

```
python app.py
```

3.

Make Predictions

Send a POST request to the Flask application to get predictions:

```
curl -X POST -H "Content-Type: application/json" -d '{"features":
[value1, value2, value3]}' http://127.0.0.1:5000/predict
```

4.

Best Practices for Machine Learning

1. **Data Quality**
   - Ensure high-quality and relevant data.
   - Handle missing values, outliers, and imbalanced data.
2. **Feature Engineering**
   - Select and create meaningful features.
   - Normalize and scale features as needed.
3. **Model Selection**
   - Experiment with different algorithms and hyperparameters.
   - Use cross-validation to evaluate model performance.
4. **Model Evaluation**
   - Use appropriate metrics for evaluation (e.g., accuracy, precision, recall).
   - Avoid overfitting by using techniques like regularization and cross-validation.
5. **Model Deployment**
   - Ensure the model is scalable and can handle real-time predictions.
   - Monitor the performance of the deployed model and retrain as necessary.

Conclusion

In this chapter, we explored the basics of machine learning, different types of machine learning algorithms, and how to build and deploy ML models using Scikit-Learn, TensorFlow, and PyTorch. By following best practices and leveraging powerful ML frameworks, you can create intelligent applications that make data-driven decisions.

In the next chapter, we will delve into data science and explore how to analyze and visualize data to gain insights and inform decision-making. Keep practicing, and let's continue your journey to becoming a proficient self-taught developer!

Chapter 16: Data Science and Data Visualization

Introduction

Data science involves extracting insights and knowledge from data through various techniques, including statistical analysis, machine learning, and data visualization. In this chapter, we will explore the basics of data science, how to analyze data using Python, and how to create visualizations to communicate your findings effectively.

The Data Science Process

The data science process typically involves the following steps:

1. **Data Collection**: Gathering relevant data from various sources.
2. **Data Cleaning**: Preparing the data by handling missing values, outliers, and inconsistencies.
3. **Exploratory Data Analysis (EDA)**: Analyzing the data to understand its structure, patterns, and relationships.
4. **Feature Engineering**: Creating and selecting features that improve model performance.
5. **Modeling**: Building and evaluating machine learning models.
6. **Visualization**: Creating visualizations to communicate insights and findings.

Setting Up Your Data Science Environment

Install Python and Jupyter Notebook
Ensure you have Python installed. Install Jupyter Notebook using pip:

```
pip install jupyter
```

1.

Install Data Science Libraries
Install popular data science libraries such as Pandas, NumPy, Matplotlib, Seaborn, and Scikit-Learn:

```
pip install pandas numpy matplotlib seaborn scikit-learn
```

2.

Data Analysis with Pandas

Pandas is a powerful data manipulation library that provides data structures like DataFrames to handle structured data.

Import Libraries and Load Data

```
import pandas as pd
```

```
# Load data

data = pd.read_csv('data/housing.csv')
```

1.

Inspect the Data
```
# Display the first few rows

print(data.head())


# Display summary statistics

print(data.describe())


# Display information about the dataset

print(data.info())
```

2.

Data Cleaning
Handle missing values and outliers:
```
# Check for missing values

print(data.isnull().sum())


# Fill missing values with the mean

data.fillna(data.mean(), inplace=True)


# Remove outliers

data = data[(data['feature1'] < data['feature1'].quantile(0.99)) &
(data['feature1'] > data['feature1'].quantile(0.01))]
```

3.

Exploratory Data Analysis (EDA)

EDA involves analyzing the data to understand its structure, patterns, and relationships.

Summary Statistics

```
# Display summary statistics for numerical columns

print(data.describe())
```

1.

Correlation Analysis

```
# Calculate the correlation matrix

correlation_matrix = data.corr()


# Display the correlation matrix

print(correlation_matrix)
```

2.

Data Visualization
Use Matplotlib and Seaborn to create visualizations:

```
import matplotlib.pyplot as plt

import seaborn as sns


# Histogram of a feature

plt.hist(data['feature1'])

plt.title('Distribution of Feature 1')

plt.xlabel('Feature 1')

plt.ylabel('Frequency')

plt.show()
```

```python
# Scatter plot of two features

plt.scatter(data['feature1'], data['feature2'])

plt.title('Feature 1 vs. Feature 2')

plt.xlabel('Feature 1')

plt.ylabel('Feature 2')

plt.show()


# Heatmap of the correlation matrix

sns.heatmap(correlation_matrix, annot=True, cmap='coolwarm')

plt.title('Correlation Matrix')

plt.show()
```

3.

Feature Engineering

Feature engineering involves creating new features and selecting the most relevant features for modeling.

Create New Features

```python
# Create a new feature based on existing features

data['new_feature'] = data['feature1'] * data['feature2']
```

1.

Feature Selection

Use feature selection techniques to identify the most relevant features:

```python
from sklearn.feature_selection import SelectKBest, f_classif


# Select the top 5 features based on ANOVA F-value
```

```python
X = data.drop('target', axis=1)

y = data['target']

selector = SelectKBest(score_func=f_classif, k=5)

X_new = selector.fit_transform(X, y)

print(selector.get_support(indices=True))
```

2.

Data Visualization

Data visualization is crucial for communicating insights and findings effectively.

Bar Plot
```python
# Bar plot of a categorical feature

sns.countplot(data['categorical_feature'])

plt.title('Distribution of Categorical Feature')

plt.xlabel('Categorical Feature')

plt.ylabel('Count')

plt.show()
```

1.

Box Plot
```python
# Box plot of a numerical feature grouped by a categorical feature

sns.boxplot(x='categorical_feature', y='numerical_feature', data=data)

plt.title('Box Plot of Numerical Feature by Categorical Feature')

plt.xlabel('Categorical Feature')

plt.ylabel('Numerical Feature')

plt.show()
```

2.

Pair Plot
```
# Pair plot of multiple features

sns.pairplot(data[['feature1', 'feature2', 'feature3', 'target']])

plt.title('Pair Plot of Features')

plt.show()
```
3.

Advanced Data Visualization with Plotly

Plotly is a graphing library that makes interactive, publication-quality graphs online.

Install Plotly
```
pip install plotly
```
1.

Create Interactive Visualizations
```
import plotly.express as px


# Scatter plot with Plotly

fig = px.scatter(data, x='feature1', y='feature2', color='target',
title='Feature 1 vs. Feature 2')

fig.show()


# Line plot with Plotly

fig = px.line(data, x='date', y='numerical_feature', title='Time
Series of Numerical Feature')

fig.show()


# Histogram with Plotly
```

```
fig = px.histogram(data, x='feature1', nbins=50, title='Distribution
of Feature 1')

fig.show()
```

2.

Best Practices for Data Science

1. **Data Quality**
   - Ensure the accuracy, completeness, and consistency of your data.
   - Handle missing values and outliers appropriately.
2. **Reproducibility**
   - Use version control to track changes to your code and data.
   - Document your data analysis process and methodologies.
3. **Visualization**
   - Use clear and concise visualizations to communicate your findings.
   - Choose the appropriate type of visualization for your data.
4. **Modeling**
   - Experiment with different algorithms and hyperparameters.
   - Use cross-validation to evaluate model performance.
5. **Interpretability**
   - Ensure that your models and visualizations are interpretable.
   - Communicate your findings effectively to stakeholders.

Conclusion

In this chapter, we explored the basics of data science, including data analysis with Pandas, exploratory data analysis (EDA), feature engineering, and data visualization. By following best practices and leveraging powerful data science tools and libraries, you can gain insights from data and inform decision-making.

In the next chapter, we will dive into advanced machine learning techniques and explore how to build and deploy sophisticated models using deep learning. Keep practicing, and let's continue your journey to becoming a proficient self-taught developer!

Chapter 17: Advanced Machine Learning Techniques

Introduction

Building on the basics of machine learning, this chapter will explore advanced techniques and algorithms that can enhance the performance and capabilities of your models. We will delve into deep learning, ensemble methods, natural language processing, and time series analysis, as well as how to deploy sophisticated models in production environments.

Deep Learning

Deep learning is a subset of machine learning that uses neural networks with many layers (deep neural networks) to model complex patterns in data.

Introduction to Neural Networks

Neural networks consist of layers of interconnected nodes (neurons) that process data and learn from it.

1. **Input Layer**: The layer that receives the input data.
2. **Hidden Layers**: Layers between the input and output layers that perform transformations on the data.
3. **Output Layer**: The layer that produces the final output.

Building Deep Neural Networks with TensorFlow

Install TensorFlow
Ensure TensorFlow is installed:
```
pip install tensorflow
```

1.

Build a Deep Neural Network
```
import tensorflow as tf

from tensorflow.keras.models import Sequential

from tensorflow.keras.layers import Dense


# Load data

(X_train, y_train), (X_test, y_test) =
tf.keras.datasets.mnist.load_data()
```

```
X_train, X_test = X_train / 255.0, X_test / 255.0


# Build the model

model = Sequential([

    Dense(128, activation='relu', input_shape=(784,)),

    Dense(128, activation='relu'),

    Dense(10, activation='softmax')

])


# Compile the model

model.compile(optimizer='adam',
loss='sparse_categorical_crossentropy', metrics=['accuracy'])


# Train the model

model.fit(X_train.reshape(-1, 784), y_train, epochs=10,
validation_split=0.2)


# Evaluate the model

test_loss, test_acc = model.evaluate(X_test.reshape(-1, 784), y_test)

print(f'Test accuracy: {test_acc}')
```

2.

Convolutional Neural Networks (CNNs)

CNNs are specialized neural networks for processing data with a grid-like structure, such as images.

Build a CNN for Image Classification

```python
from tensorflow.keras.layers import Conv2D, MaxPooling2D, Flatten


# Build the CNN model

cnn_model = Sequential([

    Conv2D(32, kernel_size=(3, 3), activation='relu', input_shape=(28,
28, 1)),

    MaxPooling2D(pool_size=(2, 2)),

    Conv2D(64, kernel_size=(3, 3), activation='relu'),

    MaxPooling2D(pool_size=(2, 2)),

    Flatten(),

    Dense(128, activation='relu'),

    Dense(10, activation='softmax')

])


# Compile the model

cnn_model.compile(optimizer='adam',
loss='sparse_categorical_crossentropy', metrics=['accuracy'])


# Train the model

cnn_model.fit(X_train.reshape(-1, 28, 28, 1), y_train, epochs=10,
validation_split=0.2)


# Evaluate the model
```

```
cnn_test_loss, cnn_test_acc = cnn_model.evaluate(X_test.reshape(-1,
28, 28, 1), y_test)

print(f'Test accuracy: {cnn_test_acc}')
```

1.

Ensemble Methods

Ensemble methods combine multiple models to improve performance.

Random Forests

Random forests are an ensemble method that combines multiple decision trees.

Train a Random Forest Model

```
from sklearn.ensemble import RandomForestClassifier

from sklearn.metrics import accuracy_score


# Load data

from sklearn.datasets import load_iris

data = load_iris()

X, y = data.data, data.target


# Split data

from sklearn.model_selection import train_test_split

X_train, X_test, y_train, y_test = train_test_split(X, y,
test_size=0.2, random_state=42)


# Train the model

rf_model = RandomForestClassifier(n_estimators=100, random_state=42)
```

```
rf_model.fit(X_train, y_train)


# Make predictions

y_pred = rf_model.predict(X_test)


# Evaluate the model

accuracy = accuracy_score(y_test, y_pred)

print(f'Random Forest accuracy: {accuracy}')
```

1.

Gradient Boosting

Gradient boosting is an ensemble method that builds models sequentially, with each model correcting the errors of the previous ones.

Train a Gradient Boosting Model
```
from sklearn.ensemble import GradientBoostingClassifier


# Train the model

gb_model = GradientBoostingClassifier(n_estimators=100,
random_state=42)

gb_model.fit(X_train, y_train)


# Make predictions

y_pred_gb = gb_model.predict(X_test)


# Evaluate the model
```

```
gb_accuracy = accuracy_score(y_test, y_pred_gb)

print(f'Gradient Boosting accuracy: {gb_accuracy}')
```

1.

Natural Language Processing (NLP)

NLP involves analyzing and modeling text data.

Text Classification with Scikit-Learn

Load and Preprocess Data

```
from sklearn.datasets import fetch_20newsgroups

from sklearn.feature_extraction.text import TfidfVectorizer


# Load data

newsgroups_train = fetch_20newsgroups(subset='train')

newsgroups_test = fetch_20newsgroups(subset='test')


# Vectorize text data

vectorizer = TfidfVectorizer()

X_train_tfidf = vectorizer.fit_transform(newsgroups_train.data)

X_test_tfidf = vectorizer.transform(newsgroups_test.data)
```

1.

Train a Text Classification Model

```
from sklearn.naive_bayes import MultinomialNB


# Train the model

nb_model = MultinomialNB()
```

```
nb_model.fit(X_train_tfidf, newsgroups_train.target)


# Make predictions

y_pred_nb = nb_model.predict(X_test_tfidf)


# Evaluate the model

nb_accuracy = accuracy_score(newsgroups_test.target, y_pred_nb)

print(f'Naive Bayes accuracy: {nb_accuracy}')
```

2.

Time Series Analysis

Time series analysis involves analyzing data points collected or recorded at specific time intervals.

Forecasting with ARIMA

Install the Required Libraries
```
pip install statsmodels
```

1.

Load and Preprocess Data
```
import pandas as pd

from statsmodels.tsa.arima_model import ARIMA


# Load data

data = pd.read_csv('data/time_series.csv', index_col='date',
parse_dates=True)


# Split data
```

```
train_data, test_data = data[:int(0.8*len(data))],
data[int(0.8*len(data)):]
```

2.

Train an ARIMA Model

```
# Train the model

arima_model = ARIMA(train_data, order=(5, 1, 0))

arima_model_fit = arima_model.fit(disp=0)


# Make predictions

forecast = arima_model_fit.forecast(steps=len(test_data))[0]


# Evaluate the model

mse = mean_squared_error(test_data, forecast)

print(f'Mean Squared Error: {mse}')
```

3.

Deploying Advanced Machine Learning Models

Deploying advanced machine learning models involves ensuring scalability, reliability, and performance.

Deploying with Docker and Kubernetes

Create a Dockerfile

```
FROM python:3.8-slim


WORKDIR /app


COPY requirements.txt requirements.txt
```

```
RUN pip install -r requirements.txt


COPY . .


CMD ["python", "app.py"]
```

1.

Build and Run the Docker Image
```
docker build -t my_ml_app .

docker run -p 5000:5000 my_ml_app
```

2.

Deploy to Kubernetes
Create a Kubernetes deployment file:
```
apiVersion: apps/v1

kind: Deployment

metadata:

  name: my-ml-app

spec:

  replicas: 3

  selector:

    matchLabels:

      app: my-ml-app

  template:

    metadata:

      labels:
```

```
      app: my-ml-app

  spec:

    containers:

    - name: my-ml-app

      image: my_ml_app:latest

      ports:

      - containerPort: 5000
```

Deploy to Kubernetes:
```
kubectl apply -f deployment.yaml
```

3.

Best Practices for Advanced Machine Learning

1. **Experimentation**
   - Continuously experiment with different models and hyperparameters.
   - Use automated tools like Grid Search and Random Search for hyperparameter tuning.
2. **Feature Engineering**
   - Create and select the most relevant features.
   - Use domain knowledge to create meaningful features.
3. **Model Interpretability**
   - Use tools like SHAP and LIME to explain model predictions.
   - Ensure that your models are interpretable and understandable.
4. **Scalability**
   - Ensure that your models can handle large-scale data.
   - Use distributed computing frameworks like Apache Spark for large-scale processing.
5. **Model Monitoring**
   - Continuously monitor the performance of deployed models.
   - Retrain models as necessary to maintain performance.

Conclusion

In this chapter, we explored advanced machine learning techniques, including deep learning, ensemble methods, natural language processing, and time series analysis. We also covered how to deploy sophisticated models using Docker and Kubernetes. By following best practices and leveraging advanced techniques, you can build and deploy powerful machine learning models that deliver significant value.

In the next chapter, we will delve into data engineering and explore how to design and build scalable data pipelines. Keep practicing, and let's continue your journey to becoming a proficient self-taught developer!

Chapter 18: Data Engineering and Scalable Data Pipelines

Introduction

Data engineering involves designing, building, and maintaining systems that allow for the collection, storage, and analysis of data at scale. It is a critical component of the data ecosystem, ensuring that data is reliable, accessible, and in a usable format for analysis and machine learning. In this chapter, we will explore the fundamentals of data engineering, including designing data pipelines, working with batch and stream processing, and using popular tools like Apache Spark, Apache Kafka, and Airflow.

Fundamentals of Data Engineering

Data engineering encompasses several key areas:

1. **Data Collection**: Gathering data from various sources.
2. **Data Storage**: Storing data in databases or data lakes.
3. **Data Processing**: Transforming and cleaning data to make it usable.
4. **Data Integration**: Combining data from different sources.
5. **Data Quality**: Ensuring the accuracy and reliability of data.
6. **Data Orchestration**: Automating and managing data workflows.

Designing Data Pipelines

A data pipeline is a series of processes that move data from one or more sources to a destination where it can be stored and analyzed.

1. **Define the Pipeline Requirements**
   - Identify the data sources and destinations.
   - Determine the data transformations and processing needed.
   - Establish data quality checks and validation steps.
   - Plan for scalability and fault tolerance.
2. **Choose the Right Tools**
   - **Batch Processing**: Suitable for processing large volumes of data at scheduled intervals.
   - **Stream Processing**: Suitable for processing data in real-time as it is generated.

Batch Processing with Apache Spark

Apache Spark is a powerful open-source engine for big data processing that supports both batch and stream processing.

Setting Up Apache Spark

1. **Install Apache Spark**
   Follow the installation instructions on the <u>Apache Spark website</u>.

Start a Spark Session

```
from pyspark.sql import SparkSession


# Create a Spark session

spark = SparkSession.builder \

    .appName("DataEngineering") \

    .getOrCreate()
```

2.

Building a Batch Processing Pipeline

Load Data
```
# Load data from a CSV file

df = spark.read.csv("data/housing.csv", header=True, inferSchema=True)
```

1.

Transform Data
```
# Perform data transformations

df = df.withColumnRenamed("feature1", "Feature1") \

       .withColumnRenamed("feature2", "Feature2")
```

2.

Aggregate Data
```
# Aggregate data

aggregated_df = df.groupBy("Feature1").agg({"Feature2": "mean"})
```

3.

Save Processed Data
```
# Save the processed data to a new CSV file
```

```
aggregated_df.write.csv("data/processed_housing.csv", header=True)
```

4.

Stream Processing with Apache Kafka

Apache Kafka is a distributed streaming platform that allows you to build real-time data pipelines and streaming applications.

Setting Up Apache Kafka

1. **Install Apache Kafka**
   Follow the installation instructions on the Apache Kafka website.

Start Kafka Server
Start the ZooKeeper and Kafka server:
```
bin/zookeeper-server-start.sh config/zookeeper.properties
```
```
bin/kafka-server-start.sh config/server.properties
```

2.

Building a Stream Processing Pipeline

Produce Messages to Kafka Topic
```
from kafka import KafkaProducer

import json


producer = KafkaProducer(bootstrap_servers='localhost:9092',
value_serializer=lambda v: json.dumps(v).encode('utf-8'))


data = {"Feature1": 1, "Feature2": 2.5}

producer.send('housing', value=data)

producer.flush()
```

1.

Consume Messages from Kafka Topic

```
from kafka import KafkaConsumer


consumer = KafkaConsumer('housing',
bootstrap_servers='localhost:9092', value_deserializer=lambda v:
json.loads(v.decode('utf-8')))


for message in consumer:

    print(message.value)
```

2.

Orchestrating Data Workflows with Apache Airflow

Apache Airflow is an open-source platform to programmatically author, schedule, and monitor workflows.

Setting Up Apache Airflow

Install Apache Airflow

```
pip install apache-airflow
```

1.

Initialize Airflow Database

```
airflow db init
```

2.

Start Airflow Web Server and Scheduler

```
airflow webserver --port 8080

airflow scheduler
```

3.

Creating an Airflow DAG

Define a DAG
Create a new Python file in the dags folder:

```python
from airflow import DAG

from airflow.operators.python_operator import PythonOperator

from datetime import datetime, timedelta


def print_hello():

    print('Hello world!')


default_args = {

    'owner': 'airflow',

    'depends_on_past': False,

    'start_date': datetime(2021, 1, 1),

    'retries': 1,

    'retry_delay': timedelta(minutes=5),

}


dag = DAG(

    'hello_world',

    default_args=default_args,

    description='A simple hello world DAG',

    schedule_interval=timedelta(days=1),

)
```

```
t1 = PythonOperator(

    task_id='print_hello',

    python_callable=print_hello,

    dag=dag,

)
```

1.
2. **Deploy and Run the DAG**
   Save the DAG file and view it in the Airflow web UI. Trigger the DAG manually or wait for the scheduled interval.

Best Practices for Data Engineering

1. **Data Quality**
   - Implement data validation and quality checks at every stage of the pipeline.
   - Monitor data quality metrics and address issues promptly.
2. **Scalability**
   - Design data pipelines to scale horizontally.
   - Use distributed computing frameworks like Apache Spark for large-scale processing.
3. **Fault Tolerance**
   - Ensure that data pipelines are fault-tolerant and can recover from failures.
   - Use retry mechanisms and logging to handle errors gracefully.
4. **Automation**
   - Automate data workflows using orchestration tools like Apache Airflow.
   - Schedule regular data processing jobs to keep data up-to-date.
5. **Documentation**
   - Document data sources, transformations, and processing steps.
   - Maintain clear and comprehensive documentation for data pipelines.

Conclusion

In this chapter, we explored the fundamentals of data engineering and how to design and build scalable data pipelines. We covered batch processing with Apache Spark, stream processing with Apache Kafka, and workflow orchestration with Apache Airflow. By following best practices and leveraging powerful data engineering tools, you can ensure that your data is reliable, accessible, and ready for analysis.

In the next chapter, we will dive into the principles of software architecture and design patterns, exploring how to build robust and maintainable software systems. Keep practicing, and let's continue your journey to becoming a proficient self-taught developer!

Chapter 19: Software Architecture and Design Patterns

Introduction

Software architecture and design patterns are essential for building robust, maintainable, and scalable software systems. Good architecture ensures that your software can evolve and adapt to changing requirements, while design patterns provide reusable solutions to common problems. In this chapter, we will explore the principles of software architecture, various architectural styles, and popular design patterns.

Principles of Software Architecture

1. **Separation of Concerns**: Divide the software into distinct sections, each responsible for a specific part of the functionality. This makes the system easier to manage and understand.
2. **Modularity**: Design the system as a collection of independent modules that can be developed, tested, and maintained separately.
3. **Scalability**: Ensure that the system can handle increased load by scaling horizontally (adding more machines) or vertically (adding more resources to a machine).
4. **Resilience**: Design the system to recover gracefully from failures, ensuring high availability and reliability.
5. **Maintainability**: Write clean, well-documented code that is easy to understand and modify.
6. **Performance**: Optimize the system to handle the required load efficiently, ensuring fast response times and low latency.

Architectural Styles

Layered Architecture
The layered architecture divides the system into layers, each responsible for a specific aspect of the functionality. Common layers include the presentation layer, business logic layer, and data access layer.

```
+---------------------+
| Presentation Layer  |
+---------------------+
| Business Logic Layer|
+---------------------+
| Data Access Layer   |
+---------------------+
```

1.

Microservices Architecture

The microservices architecture breaks down the system into small, independent services that communicate over a network. Each service is responsible for a specific business capability.

```
+--------------------+    +--------------------+
|  User Service   |       |  Order Service   |
+--------------------+    +--------------------+
|                 |       |                  |
|  Database       |       |  Database        |
+--------------------+    +--------------------+
```

2.

Event-Driven Architecture

The event-driven architecture uses events to communicate between different parts of the system. Components produce and consume events to trigger actions and responses.

```
+--------------+    +------------------+    +--------------+
| Event Source |-->| Event Processing |-->| Event Sink   |
+--------------+    +------------------+    +--------------+
```

3.

Service-Oriented Architecture (SOA)
The SOA architecture organizes the system as a collection of services that communicate using standardized interfaces and protocols.

```
+--------------+     +--------------+     +--------------+

|  Service A   |<-->|  Service B   |<-->|  Service C   |

+--------------+     +--------------+     +--------------+
```

4.

Design Patterns

1. **Creational Patterns**
   Creational patterns provide ways to create objects while hiding the creation logic, making the system more flexible and reusable.

Singleton Pattern: Ensures that a class has only one instance and provides a global point of access to it.

```python
class Singleton:

    _instance = None


    def __new__(cls, *args, **kwargs):

        if not cls._instance:

            cls._instance = super().__new__(cls, *args, **kwargs)

        return cls._instance

        o
```

Factory Pattern: Defines an interface for creating objects but allows subclasses to alter the type of objects that will be created.

```python
class ShapeFactory:

    @staticmethod

    def create_shape(type):

        if type == 'circle':
```

```
            return Circle()

        elif type == 'square':

            return Square()

        else:

            raise ValueError("Unknown shape type")
```

   o

2. **Structural Patterns**
   Structural patterns deal with the composition of classes or objects, making the system easier to design by identifying relationships.

Adapter Pattern: Allows incompatible interfaces to work together by converting the interface of a class into another interface the client expects.

```
class Adaptee:

    def specific_request(self):

        return "Adaptee behavior"



class Adapter:

    def __init__(self, adaptee):

        self.adaptee = adaptee


    def request(self):

        return self.adaptee.specific_request()
```

   o

Decorator Pattern: Adds new behavior to an object dynamically by placing it inside a special wrapper object that contains the behavior.

```
class Coffee:

    def cost(self):
```

```
            return 5


class MilkDecorator:

    def __init__(self, coffee):

        self.coffee = coffee


    def cost(self):

        return self.coffee.cost() + 2
```

   o
3. **Behavioral Patterns**
   Behavioral patterns deal with algorithms and the assignment of responsibilities between objects, making the system more flexible and efficient.

Observer Pattern: Defines a one-to-many dependency between objects so that when one object changes state, all its dependents are notified and updated automatically.

```
class Subject:

    def __init__(self):

        self._observers = []


    def attach(self, observer):

        self._observers.append(observer)


    def notify(self):

        for observer in self._observers:

            observer.update()
```

```python
class Observer:

    def update(self):

        pass
```
        o
Strategy Pattern: Defines a family of algorithms, encapsulates each one, and makes them interchangeable. This pattern lets the algorithm vary independently from the clients that use it.
```python
class Strategy:

    def execute(self, data):

        pass


class ConcreteStrategyA(Strategy):

    def execute(self, data):

        return data.lower()


class Context:

    def __init__(self, strategy):

        self.strategy = strategy


    def execute_strategy(self, data):

        return self.strategy.execute(data)
```
        o

Applying Design Patterns in Real-World Projects

1. **Identify the Problem**
   o Determine the specific problem or challenge you are facing in your project.

- Analyze the context and requirements to understand the root cause of the problem.

2. **Select the Appropriate Pattern**
   - Choose a design pattern that best addresses the identified problem.
   - Consider the trade-offs and benefits of using the chosen pattern.

3. **Implement the Pattern**
   - Apply the design pattern to your codebase, ensuring that it integrates well with the existing architecture.
   - Refactor your code to accommodate the new design pattern, if necessary.

4. **Evaluate the Solution**
   - Test the implementation to ensure that it solves the problem effectively.
   - Evaluate the impact of the design pattern on the overall system performance and maintainability.

Best Practices for Software Architecture and Design Patterns

1. **Keep It Simple**
   - Avoid over-engineering your solutions. Use design patterns only when necessary and beneficial.
   - Focus on simplicity and clarity in your architecture and design.

2. **Document Your Design**
   - Clearly document your architectural decisions and the design patterns you have implemented.
   - Provide examples and use cases to help other developers understand your design choices.

3. **Continuous Improvement**
   - Regularly review and refactor your architecture and design to adapt to changing requirements and improve performance.
   - Stay updated with the latest trends and best practices in software architecture and design patterns.

4. **Collaboration**
   - Involve your team in architectural and design discussions to leverage diverse perspectives and expertise.
   - Encourage collaboration and knowledge sharing to foster a culture of continuous learning and improvement.

Conclusion

In this chapter, we explored the principles of software architecture, various architectural styles, and popular design patterns. By understanding and applying these concepts, you can build robust, maintainable, and scalable software systems. Following best practices and continuously improving your architecture and design will help you deliver high-quality software that meets the needs of your users.

In the next chapter, we will dive into the principles of cybersecurity and explore how to build secure applications and protect your data. Keep practicing, and let's continue your journey to becoming a proficient self-taught developer!

Chapter 20: Cybersecurity and Building Secure Applications

Introduction

Cybersecurity is crucial for protecting applications and data from malicious attacks and unauthorized access. As a developer, understanding the principles of cybersecurity and implementing best practices is essential for building secure applications. In this chapter, we will explore the fundamentals of cybersecurity, common threats, and how to secure your applications through various techniques and best practices.

Fundamentals of Cybersecurity

Cybersecurity involves protecting systems, networks, and data from digital attacks. The key goals of cybersecurity include:

1. **Confidentiality**: Ensuring that data is accessible only to authorized users.
2. **Integrity**: Ensuring that data is accurate and has not been tampered with.
3. **Availability**: Ensuring that systems and data are available when needed.

Common Threats

1. **Malware**: Malicious software designed to damage or disrupt systems.
2. **Phishing**: Fraudulent attempts to obtain sensitive information by disguising as a trustworthy entity.
3. **SQL Injection**: An attack that allows attackers to execute malicious SQL statements.
4. **Cross-Site Scripting (XSS)**: An attack that injects malicious scripts into web pages viewed by other users.
5. **Denial of Service (DoS)**: An attack that overwhelms a system, making it unavailable to users.
6. **Man-in-the-Middle (MitM)**: An attack where the attacker intercepts and alters communication between two parties.

Securing Applications

Secure Coding Practices

1. **Input Validation**
   - Validate all input to ensure it is safe and expected.
   - Use whitelisting to allow only known good input.

```
# Example of input validation
```

```
def validate_input(user_input):

    if not user_input.isalnum():

        raise ValueError("Invalid input")

    return user_input
```

2.
3. **Output Encoding**
   o Encode output to prevent injection attacks such as XSS.

```
# Example of output encoding

from html import escape


def safe_output(user_input):

    return escape(user_input)
```

4.
5. **Use Secure Libraries and Frameworks**
   o Use well-maintained libraries and frameworks that follow security best practices.
   o Keep libraries and frameworks up-to-date to mitigate vulnerabilities.
6. **Authentication and Authorization**
   o Implement strong authentication mechanisms, such as multi-factor authentication (MFA).
   o Use role-based access control (RBAC) to enforce least privilege.

```
# Example of role-based access control

def has_permission(user, action):

    if user.role == 'admin' or action in user.permissions:

        return True

    return False
```

7.
8. **Encrypt Sensitive Data**

- Use encryption to protect sensitive data at rest and in transit.

```
# Example of data encryption

from cryptography.fernet import Fernet


key = Fernet.generate_key()

cipher_suite = Fernet(key)

cipher_text = cipher_suite.encrypt(b"Sensitive Data")

plain_text = cipher_suite.decrypt(cipher_text)
```

9.

Secure Development Lifecycle

1. **Threat Modeling**
   - Identify potential threats and vulnerabilities during the design phase.
   - Use threat modeling tools to assess risks and plan mitigations.
2. **Security Testing**
   - Conduct regular security testing, including penetration testing and vulnerability scanning.
   - Use automated tools to identify security issues early in the development process.
3. **Code Reviews**
   - Perform code reviews to identify security vulnerabilities and ensure adherence to secure coding practices.
   - Use static analysis tools to analyze code for security issues.
4. **Incident Response**
   - Develop an incident response plan to handle security breaches and incidents.
   - Regularly test and update the incident response plan.

Securing Web Applications

1. **Preventing SQL Injection**
   - Use parameterized queries or prepared statements to prevent SQL injection.

```
# Example of parameterized query

import sqlite3
```

```
conn = sqlite3.connect('database.db')

cursor = conn.cursor()

cursor.execute("SELECT * FROM users WHERE username = ?", (username,))
```

2.
3. **Preventing Cross-Site Scripting (XSS)**
    o   Sanitize and validate input to prevent XSS attacks.
    o   Use content security policy (CSP) headers to mitigate XSS.

```
# Example of setting CSP headers

from flask import Flask, make_response


app = Flask(__name__)


@app.after_request

def set_csp(response):

    response.headers['Content-Security-Policy'] = "default-src 'self'"

    return response
```

4.
5. **Preventing Cross-Site Request Forgery (CSRF)**
    o   Use anti-CSRF tokens to prevent CSRF attacks.

```
# Example of CSRF protection with Flask-WTF

from flask_wtf.csrf import CSRFProtect


app = Flask(__name__)
```

```
csrf = CSRFProtect(app)
```

6.
7. **Secure Session Management**
   - Use secure session cookies and ensure that they are HTTP-only and have the secure flag set.

```
# Example of setting secure session cookies in Flask

from flask import session


app.config.update(

    SESSION_COOKIE_HTTPONLY=True,

    SESSION_COOKIE_SECURE=True,

)
```

8.

Securing APIs

1. **Authentication and Authorization**
   - Use API keys, OAuth, or JWT for secure authentication and authorization.

```
# Example of JWT authentication

import jwt


token = jwt.encode({'user_id': user.id}, 'secret', algorithm='HS256')

decoded = jwt.decode(token, 'secret', algorithms=['HS256'])
```

2.
3. **Rate Limiting**
   - Implement rate limiting to prevent abuse and DoS attacks.

```
# Example of rate limiting with Flask-Limiter

from flask_limiter import Limiter


app = Flask(__name__)
limiter = Limiter(app, key_func=get_remote_address)


@app.route('/api')
@limiter.limit("5 per minute")
def api_endpoint():

    return "API response"
```

    4.
    5. **Input Validation and Sanitization**
        o Validate and sanitize input to prevent injection attacks and ensure data integrity.

```
# Example of input validation for an API

from marshmallow import Schema, fields, ValidationError


class InputSchema(Schema):

    name = fields.Str(required=True)


def validate_input(data):

    try:

        InputSchema().load(data)

    except ValidationError as err:
```

```
            raise ValueError("Invalid input")
```

6.
7. **Use HTTPS**
   o Use HTTPS to encrypt data in transit and prevent eavesdropping and
     man-in-the-middle attacks.

```python
        # Example of forcing HTTPS in Flask

from flask import redirect, request, url_for


@app.before_request

def before_request():

    if request.url.startswith('http://'):

        return redirect(request.url.replace('http://', 'https://', 1))
```

8.

Monitoring and Logging

1. **Implement Logging**
   o Log important events and errors for monitoring and auditing purposes.
   o Use a centralized logging solution to aggregate and analyze logs.

```python
        # Example of logging in Python

import logging


logging.basicConfig(level=logging.INFO)

logger = logging.getLogger(__name__)


logger.info("This is an info message")
```

2.
3. **Monitor Security Metrics**
   - Monitor security metrics, such as failed login attempts and unusual activity, to detect potential threats.
   - Use monitoring tools and dashboards to track security metrics in real-time.
4. **Intrusion Detection and Prevention**
   - Implement intrusion detection and prevention systems (IDPS) to detect and block malicious activity.
   - Regularly review IDPS logs and alerts to identify potential security incidents.

Best Practices for Cybersecurity

1. **Stay Updated**
   - Regularly update software, libraries, and dependencies to patch known vulnerabilities.
   - Stay informed about the latest security threats and best practices.
2. **Educate and Train**
   - Educate and train developers and employees on cybersecurity best practices.
   - Foster a security-first culture within your organization.
3. **Regular Security Audits**
   - Conduct regular security audits to identify and address vulnerabilities.
   - Use third-party security assessments to validate the effectiveness of your security measures.
4. **Implement Defense in Depth**
   - Use multiple layers of security controls to protect your applications and data.
   - Implement both preventive and detective security measures.

Conclusion

In this chapter, we explored the fundamentals of cybersecurity, common threats, and how to secure applications through various techniques and best practices. By understanding and implementing these principles, you can build secure applications that protect sensitive data and resist attacks. Following best practices and staying updated with the latest security trends will help you maintain a strong security posture.

In the next chapter, we will delve into the principles of DevOps and explore how to streamline the development and deployment process to deliver software faster and more reliably. Keep practicing, and let's continue your journey to becoming a proficient self-taught developer!

Chapter 21: DevOps: Streamlining Development and Deployment

Introduction

DevOps is a set of practices that aims to automate and integrate the processes between software development and IT operations teams, enabling them to build, test, and release software faster and more reliably. By adopting DevOps principles and practices, organizations can improve collaboration, reduce time to market, and ensure higher quality software. In this chapter, we will explore the core principles of DevOps, continuous integration (CI), continuous delivery/deployment (CD), infrastructure as code (IaC), and monitoring and logging.

Core Principles of DevOps

1. **Collaboration**: Enhance communication and collaboration between development, operations, and other teams.
2. **Automation**: Automate repetitive tasks to improve efficiency and reduce human error.
3. **Continuous Integration and Continuous Deployment (CI/CD)**: Continuously integrate and deploy code changes to ensure faster and more reliable releases.
4. **Infrastructure as Code (IaC)**: Manage and provision infrastructure through code to ensure consistency and repeatability.
5. **Monitoring and Logging**: Continuously monitor applications and infrastructure to detect issues early and maintain performance.

Continuous Integration (CI)

Continuous integration involves automatically integrating code changes from multiple developers into a shared repository, followed by automated builds and tests to detect issues early.

Setting Up CI with GitHub Actions

GitHub Actions is a CI/CD tool integrated with GitHub that allows you to automate workflows.

1. **Create a GitHub Repository**
   Create a new repository on GitHub for your project.

Add a CI Workflow

In your repository, create a `.github/workflows/ci.yml` file with the following content:

```
name: CI

on:
```

```yaml
  push:
    branches:
      - main
  pull_request:
    branches:
      - main

jobs:
  build:
    runs-on: ubuntu-latest

    steps:
    - uses: actions/checkout@v2
    - name: Set up Python
      uses: actions/setup-python@v2
      with:
        python-version: '3.8'
    - name: Install dependencies
      run: |
        python -m pip install --upgrade pip
        pip install -r requirements.txt
    - name: Run tests
      run: |
```

```
    pytest
```

2. This workflow runs on every push to the main branch and on pull requests. It sets up Python, installs dependencies, and runs tests using `pytest`.

Commit and Push Changes

Commit and push your changes to trigger the CI workflow:

```
git add .
```

```
git commit -m "Set up CI with GitHub Actions"
```

```
git push origin main
```

3.
4. **View CI Results**

   Open your GitHub repository and navigate to the "Actions" tab to view the results of your CI workflow.

Continuous Delivery/Deployment (CD)

Continuous delivery involves automatically deploying code changes to staging environments after they pass all tests, while continuous deployment extends this to production environments. This ensures that new features and bug fixes are delivered quickly and reliably.

Setting Up CD with GitHub Actions

Extend your CI workflow to include deployment steps.

Add Deployment Steps

Update your `.github/workflows/ci.yml` file to include deployment steps:

```
name: CI/CD


on:

  push:

    branches:

      - main

  pull_request:

    branches:
```

```yaml
      - main


jobs:
  build:
    runs-on: ubuntu-latest


    steps:
    - uses: actions/checkout@v2
    - name: Set up Python
      uses: actions/setup-python@v2
      with:
        python-version: '3.8'
    - name: Install dependencies
      run: |
        python -m pip install --upgrade pip
        pip install -r requirements.txt
    - name: Run tests
      run: |
        pytest
    - name: Deploy to Heroku
      env:
        HEROKU_API_KEY: ${{ secrets.HEROKU_API_KEY }}
      run: |
```

```
        git remote add heroku
https://git.heroku.com/your-heroku-app.git

        git push heroku main
```

1. This workflow includes a deployment step to Heroku. You need to add your Heroku API key as a secret in your GitHub repository settings.
2. **Add Heroku API Key to GitHub Secrets**
   Go to your GitHub repository settings, navigate to "Secrets," and add a new secret named `HEROKU_API_KEY` with your Heroku API key.

Commit and Push Changes
Commit and push your changes to trigger the CI/CD workflow:
```
git add .

git commit -m "Set up CD with GitHub Actions"

git push origin main
```

3.
4. **View Deployment Results**
   Open your GitHub repository and navigate to the "Actions" tab to view the results of your CI/CD workflow.

Infrastructure as Code (IaC)

Infrastructure as code (IaC) involves managing and provisioning infrastructure through code and automation tools. This ensures consistency, repeatability, and scalability.

Using Terraform for IaC

Terraform is an open-source IaC tool that allows you to define and provision infrastructure using a declarative configuration language.

1. **Install Terraform**
   Follow the installation instructions on the Terraform website.

Create a Terraform Configuration
Create a `main.tf` file with the following content:
```
provider "aws" {

  region = "us-west-2"

}
```

```
resource "aws_instance" "example" {

  ami           = "ami-0c55b159cbfafe1f0"

  instance_type = "t2.micro"


  tags = {

    Name = "example-instance"

  }

}
```

2. This configuration defines an AWS EC2 instance.

Initialize Terraform
Initialize Terraform to download the necessary plugins:
```
terraform init
```

3.

Apply the Configuration
Apply the configuration to provision the infrastructure:
```
terraform apply
```

4.

Manage Infrastructure Changes
Use Terraform to manage and apply changes to your infrastructure. For example, to change the instance type:
```
resource "aws_instance" "example" {

  ami           = "ami-0c55b159cbfafe1f0"

  instance_type = "t2.small"


  tags = {
```

```
    Name = "example-instance"

  }

}
```

Apply the changes:
```
terraform apply
```

    5.

Monitoring and Logging

Monitoring and logging are essential for ensuring the performance and reliability of your applications and infrastructure.

Using Prometheus and Grafana

Prometheus is an open-source monitoring and alerting toolkit, and Grafana is an open-source platform for monitoring and observability.

1. **Install Prometheus**
   Follow the installation instructions on the Prometheus website.

Configure Prometheus
Create a `prometheus.yml` configuration file:
```
global:

  scrape_interval: 15s


scrape_configs:

  - job_name: 'prometheus'

    static_configs:

      - targets: ['localhost:9090']
```

    2.

Start Prometheus
Start Prometheus using the configuration file:
```
./prometheus --config.file=prometheus.yml
```

3.
4. **Install Grafana**
   Follow the installation instructions on the Grafana website.
5. **Configure Grafana**
   Add Prometheus as a data source in Grafana and create dashboards to visualize metrics.

Best Practices for DevOps

1. **Automate Everything**
   - Automate builds, tests, deployments, and infrastructure provisioning.
   - Use CI/CD pipelines to ensure code changes are integrated and deployed continuously.
2. **Version Control**
   - Use version control for both code and infrastructure.
   - Maintain a clean and organized repository structure.
3. **Monitoring and Logging**
   - Implement comprehensive monitoring and logging for applications and infrastructure.
   - Set up alerts to detect and respond to issues promptly.
4. **Security**
   - Implement security best practices, such as encryption, access controls, and regular security audits.
   - Use tools and services to scan for vulnerabilities and ensure compliance.
5. **Collaboration**
   - Foster a culture of collaboration between development and operations teams.
   - Use collaboration tools to streamline communication and project management.

Conclusion

In this chapter, we explored the core principles of DevOps and how to implement continuous integration (CI), continuous delivery/deployment (CD), infrastructure as code (IaC), and monitoring and logging. By adopting DevOps practices, you can streamline your development and deployment processes, improve collaboration, and ensure higher quality software.

In the next chapter, we will delve into mobile app development, exploring how to build cross-platform mobile applications using frameworks like React Native and Flutter. Keep practicing, and let's continue your journey to becoming a proficient self-taught developer!

Chapter 22: Cross-Platform Mobile App Development

Introduction

With the rise of smartphones, mobile app development has become a crucial skill for developers. Cross-platform frameworks allow developers to build mobile applications for both iOS and Android using a single codebase, saving time and effort. In this chapter, we will explore two popular cross-platform frameworks: React Native and Flutter. We will cover the basics of each framework, setting up the development environment, and building a simple mobile application.

Introduction to React Native

React Native is a popular framework for building mobile applications using JavaScript and React. It allows developers to use the same design principles and components as React while providing access to native mobile features.

Setting Up React Native

1. **Install Node.js and npm**
   Ensure you have Node.js and npm (Node Package Manager) installed. Download and install them from Node.js.

Install Expo CLI
Expo CLI is a tool for developing React Native apps quickly.
```
npm install -g expo-cli
```

2.

Create a New React Native Project
Use Expo CLI to create a new project:
```
expo init MyReactNativeApp

cd MyReactNativeApp

expo start
```

3.

This command sets up a new React Native application and starts the development server. Follow the instructions to open the app on your device using the Expo Go app.

Building a Simple React Native App

Create a Basic Component

Open App.js and modify it to create a simple component:

```
import React, { useState } from 'react';

import { StyleSheet, Text, View, TextInput, Button, FlatList } from
'react-native';


export default function App() {

    const [task, setTask] = useState('');

    const [tasks, setTasks] = useState([]);


    const addTask = () => {

        setTasks([...tasks, { key: Math.random().toString(), value:
task }]);

        setTask('');

    };


    return (

        <View style={styles.container}>

            <Text style={styles.title}>To-Do List</Text>

            <TextInput

                style={styles.input}

                placeholder="Enter a new task"

                value={task}

                onChangeText={setTask}
```

```
        />

        <Button title="Add Task" onPress={addTask} />

        <FlatList

            data={tasks}

            renderItem={({ item }) => <Text
style={styles.task}>{item.value}</Text>}

        />

    </View>

    );

}


const styles = StyleSheet.create({

    container: {

        flex: 1,

        backgroundColor: '#fff',

        alignItems: 'center',

        justifyContent: 'center',

        padding: 20,

    },

    title: {

        fontSize: 24,

        fontWeight: 'bold',

    },
```

```
input: {

    height: 40,

    borderColor: 'gray',

    borderWidth: 1,

    marginBottom: 10,

    paddingHorizontal: 10,

    width: '100%',

},

task: {

    padding: 10,

    fontSize: 18,

    borderBottomColor: 'gray',

    borderBottomWidth: 1,

    width: '100%',

},

});
```

1.

Run the App

Run your app using the Expo CLI:

```
expo start
```

2. Use the Expo Go app on your device to scan the QR code and view the app.

Introduction to Flutter

Flutter is a UI toolkit from Google for building natively compiled applications for mobile, web, and desktop from a single codebase. It uses the Dart programming language.

Setting Up Flutter

1. **Install Flutter**
   Download and install Flutter from the <u>official Flutter website</u>.

Create a New Flutter Project
Use the Flutter CLI to create a new project:

```
flutter create my_flutter_app

cd my_flutter_app

flutter run
```

2. This command sets up a new Flutter application and runs it on the connected device or emulator.

Building a Simple Flutter App

Create a Basic Component
Open lib/main.dart and modify it to create a simple component:

```
import 'package:flutter/material.dart';


void main() => runApp(MyApp());


class MyApp extends StatelessWidget {

  @override

  Widget build(BuildContext context) {

    return MaterialApp(

      title: 'To-Do List',

      theme: ThemeData(

        primarySwatch: Colors.blue,

      ),

      home: ToDoList(),
```

```dart
      );
    }
  }


class ToDoList extends StatefulWidget {
  @override
  _ToDoListState createState() => _ToDoListState();
}


class _ToDoListState extends State<ToDoList> {
  final List<String> _tasks = [];
  final TextEditingController _controller = TextEditingController();


  void _addTask() {
    setState(() {
      _tasks.add(_controller.text);
      _controller.clear();
    });
  }


  @override
  Widget build(BuildContext context) {
    return Scaffold(
```

```
appBar: AppBar(
  title: Text('To-Do List'),
),
body: Column(
  children: <Widget>[
    Padding(
      padding: const EdgeInsets.all(16.0),
      child: TextField(
        controller: _controller,
        decoration: InputDecoration(labelText: 'Enter a new
task'),
      ),
    ),
    ElevatedButton(
      onPressed: _addTask,
      child: Text('Add Task'),
    ),
    Expanded(
      child: ListView.builder(
        itemCount: _tasks.length,
        itemBuilder: (ctx, index) {
          return ListTile(
            title: Text(_tasks[index]),
```

```
                  );
                },
              ),
            ),
          ],
        ),
      ),
    );
  }
}
```

1.

Run the App
Run your app using the Flutter CLI:

```
flutter run
```

2. This will launch the app on your connected device or emulator.

Comparing React Native and Flutter

Development Experience

- **React Native**: Leverages existing knowledge of JavaScript and React. Uses the vast ecosystem of npm packages.
- **Flutter**: Uses Dart, which may require learning a new language. Provides a comprehensive set of widgets and tools out of the box.

Performance

- **React Native**: Good performance with a bridge to native modules, but may require optimization for complex apps.
- **Flutter**: Excellent performance with a compiled binary and direct access to native components.

Community and Ecosystem

- **React Native**: Large community and mature ecosystem with many third-party libraries.

- **Flutter**: Growing community with strong support from Google and an increasing number of third-party packages.

Best Practices for Mobile App Development

1. **Code Organization**
   - Keep your code modular and organized.
   - Separate business logic from UI components.
2. **State Management**
   - Use state management libraries (e.g., Redux for React Native, Provider for Flutter) to handle complex state.
   - Keep the state as minimal as possible and derive data when needed.
3. **Navigation**
   - Use navigation libraries (e.g., React Navigation for React Native, Navigator for Flutter) for managing app navigation.
   - Plan your navigation structure and routes.
4. **Performance Optimization**
   - Optimize images and assets.
   - Avoid unnecessary re-renders and rebuilds.
   - Use profiling tools to identify and fix performance bottlenecks.
5. **Testing**
   - Write unit tests for your components and business logic.
   - Use integration tests to verify the app's functionality.
6. **User Experience**
   - Follow platform-specific design guidelines (Material Design for Android, Human Interface Guidelines for iOS).
   - Ensure your app is responsive and handles different screen sizes.

Conclusion

In this chapter, we explored cross-platform mobile app development using React Native and Flutter. Both frameworks enable you to build powerful mobile applications for iOS and Android with a single codebase. By following best practices and leveraging the strengths of each framework, you can create high-quality, performant, and user-friendly mobile apps.

In the next chapter, we will delve into the principles of data engineering and explore how to design and build scalable data pipelines. Keep practicing, and let's continue your journey to becoming a proficient self-taught developer!

Chapter 23: Data Engineering and Scalable Data Pipelines

Introduction

Data engineering involves designing, building, and maintaining systems that allow for the collection, storage, and analysis of data at scale. It is a critical component of the data ecosystem, ensuring that data is reliable, accessible, and in a usable format for analysis and machine learning. In this chapter, we will explore the fundamentals of data engineering, including designing data pipelines, working with batch and stream processing, and using popular tools like Apache Spark, Apache Kafka, and Airflow.

Fundamentals of Data Engineering

Data engineering encompasses several key areas:

1. **Data Collection**: Gathering data from various sources.
2. **Data Storage**: Storing data in databases or data lakes.
3. **Data Processing**: Transforming and cleaning data to make it usable.
4. **Data Integration**: Combining data from different sources.
5. **Data Quality**: Ensuring the accuracy and reliability of data.
6. **Data Orchestration**: Automating and managing data workflows.

Designing Data Pipelines

A data pipeline is a series of processes that move data from one or more sources to a destination where it can be stored and analyzed.

1. **Define the Pipeline Requirements**
    - Identify the data sources and destinations.
    - Determine the data transformations and processing needed.
    - Establish data quality checks and validation steps.
    - Plan for scalability and fault tolerance.
2. **Choose the Right Tools**
    - **Batch Processing**: Suitable for processing large volumes of data at scheduled intervals.
    - **Stream Processing**: Suitable for processing data in real-time as it is generated.

Batch Processing with Apache Spark

Apache Spark is a powerful open-source engine for big data processing that supports both batch and stream processing.

Setting Up Apache Spark

1. **Install Apache Spark**
   Follow the installation instructions on the Apache Spark website.

Start a Spark Session

```
from pyspark.sql import SparkSession


# Create a Spark session

spark = SparkSession.builder \

    .appName("DataEngineering") \

    .getOrCreate()
```

2.

Building a Batch Processing Pipeline

Load Data

```
# Load data from a CSV file

df = spark.read.csv("data/housing.csv", header=True, inferSchema=True)
```

1.

Transform Data

```
# Perform data transformations

df = df.withColumnRenamed("feature1", "Feature1") \

        .withColumnRenamed("feature2", "Feature2")
```

2.

Aggregate Data

```
# Aggregate data

aggregated_df = df.groupBy("Feature1").agg({"Feature2": "mean"})
```

3.

Save Processed Data

```
# Save the processed data to a new CSV file

aggregated_df.write.csv("data/processed_housing.csv", header=True)
```

4.

Stream Processing with Apache Kafka

Apache Kafka is a distributed streaming platform that allows you to build real-time data pipelines and streaming applications.

Setting Up Apache Kafka

1. **Install Apache Kafka**
   Follow the installation instructions on the Apache Kafka website.

Start Kafka Server

Start the ZooKeeper and Kafka server:

```
bin/zookeeper-server-start.sh config/zookeeper.properties

bin/kafka-server-start.sh config/server.properties
```

2.

Building a Stream Processing Pipeline

Produce Messages to Kafka Topic

```python
from kafka import KafkaProducer

import json


producer = KafkaProducer(bootstrap_servers='localhost:9092',
value_serializer=lambda v: json.dumps(v).encode('utf-8'))


data = {"Feature1": 1, "Feature2": 2.5}

producer.send('housing', value=data)

producer.flush()
```

1.

Consume Messages from Kafka Topic

```
from kafka import KafkaConsumer


consumer = KafkaConsumer('housing',
bootstrap_servers='localhost:9092', value_deserializer=lambda v:
json.loads(v.decode('utf-8')))


for message in consumer:

    print(message.value)
```

2.

Orchestrating Data Workflows with Apache Airflow

Apache Airflow is an open-source platform to programmatically author, schedule, and monitor workflows.

Setting Up Apache Airflow

Install Apache Airflow
```
pip install apache-airflow
```

1.

Initialize Airflow Database
```
airflow db init
```

2.

Start Airflow Web Server and Scheduler
```
airflow webserver --port 8080

airflow scheduler
```

3.

Creating an Airflow DAG

Define a DAG
Create a new Python file in the dags folder:

```python
from airflow import DAG

from airflow.operators.python_operator import PythonOperator

from datetime import datetime, timedelta


def print_hello():

    print('Hello world!')


default_args = {

    'owner': 'airflow',

    'depends_on_past': False,

    'start_date': datetime(2021, 1, 1),

    'retries': 1,

    'retry_delay': timedelta(minutes=5),

}


dag = DAG(

    'hello_world',

    default_args=default_args,

    description='A simple hello world DAG',

    schedule_interval=timedelta(days=1),

)
```

```
t1 = PythonOperator(

    task_id='print_hello',

    python_callable=print_hello,

    dag=dag,

)
```

1.
2. **Deploy and Run the DAG**
   Save the DAG file and view it in the Airflow web UI. Trigger the DAG manually or wait for the scheduled interval.

Best Practices for Data Engineering

1. **Data Quality**
   - Implement data validation and quality checks at every stage of the pipeline.
   - Monitor data quality metrics and address issues promptly.
2. **Scalability**
   - Design data pipelines to scale horizontally.
   - Use distributed computing frameworks like Apache Spark for large-scale processing.
3. **Fault Tolerance**
   - Ensure that data pipelines are fault-tolerant and can recover from failures.
   - Use retry mechanisms and logging to handle errors gracefully.
4. **Automation**
   - Automate data workflows using orchestration tools like Apache Airflow.
   - Schedule regular data processing jobs to keep data up-to-date.
5. **Documentation**
   - Document data sources, transformations, and processing steps.
   - Maintain clear and comprehensive documentation for data pipelines.

Conclusion

In this chapter, we explored the fundamentals of data engineering and how to design and build scalable data pipelines. We covered batch processing with Apache Spark, stream processing with Apache Kafka, and workflow orchestration with Apache Airflow. By following best practices and leveraging powerful data engineering tools, you can ensure that your data is reliable, accessible, and ready for analysis.

In the next chapter, we will delve into advanced topics in machine learning, exploring how to build and deploy sophisticated models. Keep practicing, and let's continue your journey to becoming a proficient self-taught developer!

www.ingramcontent.com/pod-product-compliance
Lightning Source LLC
Chambersburg PA
CBHW071246050326
40690CB00011B/2279